C000133382

Staging the Story

New Plays
for Worship and
Church Gatherings

SALLY ARMOUR WOTTON

Anglican Book Centre
Toronto, Canada

UNITED CHURCH PUBLISHING HOUSE
Toronto, Canada

Prologue

A play provides what we want to say. But acting is, by definition, showing, not telling. Therefore how a play is done is at least as important as the script. *Staging the Story* suggests:

- how its readers can adapt each script to a variety of church spaces using space to its fullest potential
- how to create interesting stage pictures with the actors/players
- how to make use of movement and improvisation for entrances and exits, providing crowd scenes where none are indicated in the script
- how to employ colour, fabric, and symbols effectively

The Workshop is written for directors and actors. It gives directions for preparing the actors through games and processes, assisting actors to be seen and heard, and developing characters simply. This chapter introduces techniques for good reading skills that connect the reader and the listener, and provides exercises for voice, breath, and psychological warm-up.

I have attempted to familiarize the reader with the language of the theatre by using theatre terminology throughout the book.

I hope that these plays, with their variety of staging approaches, will provide the means for church communities to discover new insights in old stories. Some of the plays are for use during a worship service—to dramatize a scripture reading or to replace the sermon with drama. Others are short, open-ended pieces that would spark discussion at a meeting.

As in all art it is the process that is the true art. The product, in our case the play, is simply the last step in the process. So the growth and inspiration gained by the director and actors is as important as that experienced by the audience.

When using these plays as liturgical drama remember the drama is always a part of a whole. Ideally, your drama should be conceived together with other planners of a worship service or event, or meeting so that the drama becomes an integral part of the whole liturgy.

CREATING A SCRIPT

Because this book is about how a play is done I want to point out that there are ways to create a script without writing it, by simply staging the scripture itself. Here is an example.

Luke 9:1–6

Scripture drama any time of the year
Performance time: 3 to 4 minutes

CHARACTERS:
Narrator
Jesus
Twelve Apostles (give or take a few)

PROPS:
A coat for each apostle
Some walking sticks and/or rolled umbrellas
Some lunch bags or pails
Some tin cups
Some wallets

TREATMENT AND SETTING:
This can be done effectively with adults or children or a mix of both, preferably in modern dress. Place the Narrator in the pulpit or to one side where he or she can see the action. If the action takes place at the top of the chancel step, have Jesus enter from somewhere up stage. The Apostles could enter from the front pew where all of their props can be placed.

NARRATOR: One day Jesus called together his twelve apostles…

(Twelve enter from front pew and gather in a stage picture in front of Jesus.)

NARRATOR: and gave them authority over all demons—power to cast them out—and to heal all diseases.

(Jesus stretches out hands over them and they react visually to the Narrator's words.)

NARRATOR: Then he sent them away to tell everyone about the coming of the realm of God and to heal the sick.

(The twelve put on coats, gather all other props, then freeze in a movement stage picture in the centre aisle.)

JESUS: Don't even take along a walking stick,

(Those with walking sticks or umbrellas react to

Jesus, take their sticks back to the front pew, and return to the stage picture.)

JESUS: nor a beggar's bag,

(Those with tin cups react to Jesus and repeat the action of those with walking sticks.)

JESUS: nor food,

(Those with food—react as above.)

JESUS: nor money,

(Those with wallets—react as above.)

JESUS: nor even an extra coat.

(All twelve react and take their coats back to the pew. They then form a listening stage picture around Jesus.)

JESUS: Be a guest in only one home at each village. If the people of a town won't listen to you when you enter it, turn around and leave, demonstrating God's anger against it by shaking its dust from your feet as you go.

NARRATOR: So they began their circuit of the villages,

(The twelve move through the nave knocking on the ends of a few pews and "shaking dust from their feet" ending in the centre aisle at twelve different pews with arms up high in a freeze position of knocking.)

NARRATOR: preaching the Good News and healing the sick. *(to the congregation)* Please stand to exchange the peace.

NARRATOR: The peace of God be always with you *(or whatever phrase your congregation uses and the response)*.

(The actors exchange the peace with those whose pew they are standing near and perhaps join that pew for the remainder of the service.)

Doing drama is inherently an exercise in building community. An actor or two or more (sometimes many more) and a director interpret a playwright's words in rehearsal and combine this effort with the work of other worship planners to share with the congregation and receive their response. In my experience, this evolving community-building process can be high art. And it is tremendously rewarding.

The plays in this book are organized around seasonal themes, though several of the plays could be done at any time of the year. Some may help a community to celebrate the spring time highs of resurrection and new birth. Others give hope and healing for the doubting darker days of autumn. Still others inspire us to act for justice in the world while life prepares to begin anew buried deep within the winter earth. Many of the plays simply tell our biblical story with humour and dramatic insight, while others are reflections on the issues and themes in our lives. They are our dramatic gospel stories.

The Workshop

This takes one hour and a half to two-and-a-half hours depending on the number of participants.

INTRODUCTION

Two things all actors (professional and nonprofessional, young and old) have in common are a love of performing for others and a fear of performing for others. As an actor's experience increases, the love and enjoyment dominate the experience. But the fear never goes away completely. Therefore, exercises that promote relaxation, strength, and confidence are as important as learning lines.

In fact, there is nothing as important for acquiring the skills of drama as building confidence. I suggest that the first rehearsal for a drama be a workshop along the lines of the one described here. You can then ask the players to do certain of the exercises daily on their own. A warm-up game is beneficial before each rehearsal as a means of getting the players out of their heads and in contact with one another in a non-threatening and fun way.

One advantage of beginning with a theatre games workshop is to be able to call upon the games in the middle of a rehearsal. It is damaging to an actor's confidence to receive a lot of personal criticism. When one player needs help, stop the rehearsal and have them all play the appropriate skill-learning game. This may solve the problem while benefiting the entire cast.

Confidence comes from repeated positive experience. Lack of confidence results in the actor's nervous fear over-balancing his or her enjoyment. This causes the actor to physically retreat, turning the body away from the congregation, mumbling words and "getting through it" as quickly as possible. Some nervousness is beneficial as it gives a performance energy, but the goal is to have the exciting anticipation over-balance the nervous dread. Theatre games build confidence because they are non-threatening mini-performances.

BREATH

In addition to fun and games, an actor needs to re-learn to breath in order to nurture the body, to readjust focus from self to a wider reality, and to be heard! Unfortunately, very early in life we all develop stressful tensions that affect our breathing habits.

Breath is vital to life and also to voice. It is a fact that with years of proper breathing our voice is the part of our anatomy that will last the longest. It is sad that when we affect the voice of an elder we speak from the throat to produce the sound most commonly associated with older people. This is because even the minor stresses of our lives cause us to develop the habit, over the years, of breathing shallowly forcing the throat, chest, and back muscles to do the work of voice production. Well-trained actors have strong, clear voices well into their eighties and even nineties, if their other life habits haven't stopped them breathing altogether.

Breath is our life force. We need to inhale it deep into the centre of ourselves, down to our diaphragm. The diaphragm is a cone-shaped, muscular partition that divides the body in half just below the waist. When we inhale, the weight of our breath flattens the cone and when we exhale the diaphragm springs into a cone shape again propelling our breath up and out. We can, of course, speak only on the exhale (try speaking when you are inhaling) and if we have breathed down to the diaphragm our voice will ride effortlessly up through our body on the exhale, untouched by any other muscles until it reaches our mouth. Here the voice is enunciated into clear sound by the jaw, lips, and tongue. This is a natural function of the body but, sadly, not necessarily a familiar one for most people.

Relearning to breath (as babies we were masters) can greatly relieve our tensions and psychological blocks that are often caused by focusing on fears and anxieties. Filling our bodies with breath and allowing our spoken thoughts to ride out on this breath is a liberating experience. It is also the only way we will be heard from a distance.

Drawing in the air around us is a primary means of sharing life with the universe. Our breathing and the breath of God become one. Associating spirit with breath widens our focus and can begin to rid us of some of our self-conscious fears and the blocks they cause.

TO BEGIN

Director and players sit in a circle so that all may see one another during these games and exercises.

FACE WARM-UP

1. Increase circulation by massaging the entire face from the jaw to the top of the head, applying pressure in small circular motions with the fingertips.

2. Then, stretch your lips, tongue, and jaw muscles in all four directions as hard and far as possible. Try to touch your tongue to your nose. Try to touch your lips, jaw, and tongue to your right ear and then to your left ear. Yawn as widely as you can.

3. End by releasing air through loosely closed lips to see if your jaw and mouth area are relaxed. If you don't sound like a horse, there is still tightness, so try again.

This warm-up exercise is good for anyone engaged in speaking publicly, even from the pulpit (although best done out of the congregation's view) and should be done regularly to strengthen the muscles needed for enunciation.

BREATHING EXERCISE A

Ask everyone to find a space on the floor where each can lie down on his or her back.

1. Remove shoes, and loosen tight collars and anything else that is physically restrictive or uncomfortable.

2. Place a weight (a large Bible or hymn book would be about right) on each person's belly (diaphragm area).

3. Ask everyone to breathe normally as you and they watch the books for an up-and-down motion. This will indicate whether or not the breath is getting down to the diaphragm.

Ask them to continue this exercise at home until they can breathe down to their centres easily and at will. A variation on this is to work with a partner with one person's head in place of a book resting on the other person's belly. Another variation is to sit on a firm chair with the heavy book resting against the belly.

BREATHING EXERCISE B

This is a meditation process. It can follow the above exercise immediately if the players are ready for it. Children under sixteen will have had enough breathing at this point, but if the players are older and are able to breathe from their diaphragms, carry on. The leader could say something like the following (after giving each instruction, allow the participants time to follow through and watch them as they do so).

1. As in prayer, your eyes may be open or closed, whichever enhances your concentration and relaxation.

2. Mentally check your body for any tight, tense areas. This could be the shoulders, the neck, hips, face, hands, anywhere. The habits of tension form in different places for different people. Tighten those tense muscles as tightly as you can, one area at a time, and then release them.

3. Concentrate on your normal breathing. Recall in your mind an actual place where you have felt completely at ease and at peace with the world (not in your bed, this is relaxation for energy not for sleep). A fireplace or the sun or some other form of fire is often present in a person's peaceful place. Keep this image in the back of your mind during the rest of the exercise.

4. We are at liberty to put our minds anywhere we wish. Most of us imagine our minds to be near our brains. Try to imagine that your mind or command centre is in the center of your body. This will better integrate action commands and breath. Sometimes, it is helpful in the imagining process to give your mind a shape or colour.

5. Now return to focusing on your normal breathing. Allow the exhale to escape through relaxed lips. Be aware of the feeling of the 'fffff' sound of pure breath. We breath at our own pace. Ignore the sounds around you and focus on your own breath. When you are ready send a mental command to the centre of your body for sound. Add energy to your breath and produce vowel sounds— "ahhh," "ooo," "eee," "aaa"—slowly sounding each vowel on a separate exhale. It is not a contest; do not sustain the sound for your full breath. Allow your body to fill each time with air when it is ready; don't force yourself to inhale. Resist listening to the sounds—yours and those around you—and focus on the feeling of your own sound coming from deep inside you. Note the difference in feeling between sound and pure breath. We are used to thinking of sound as aural, something we hear, but in order to properly integrate our sound with our breath we must be able to feel sound to shift sound from aural to tactile. Become aware of how you were breathing before trying this exercise and register any new experiences. Note any tensions that occur in your body any time during this exercise and tighten and release them.

6. Slowly bring yourself to a sitting position and do not get up until you are ready. This exercise often causes dizziness from the unaccustomed extra oxygen. When you are ready, come to an upright position either sitting or standing with a long spine, relaxed muscles, and feet slightly apart. Maintain your relaxed state. Envision your exhaling breath as a stream of energy moving upward fueled by your mind and coming from your centre. Repeat your vowel sounds again, one at a time on an exhale, with increasing energy. End this exercise with an improvised sentence uttered with full breath and full energy.

Breathing exercises can be done from time to time in a shortened form with a cast that is familiar with the breathing meditation. Actors can be seated on hard chairs. Remind them to recall their peaceful place and focus on their deep natural breathing. Then begin the vowel sounds, gradually adding energy. This is a good warm-up before rehearsals.

THEATRE GAMES AND IMPROVISATION

The basic structure of an improvisation is the who, what, and where assigned to the actors by the "audience" (which may be half the group or, if it is a small cast, you as leader). All action and dialogue proceeds out of that structure.

The first key to success in theatre games, as in all improvisation, is to learn to trust your first thoughts, resisting the strong urge to edit what comes into your mind. Letting go of the editing process is scary because from an early age we are taught to give careful consideration and the "right" answer at all times. However, once you are able to let go, you will find energy, pace, and originality in both your spoken and body language that will be satisfying, if not exhilarating.

The second key to success in theatre games is to avoid creative blocking. If your partner on "stage" suggests a who, a what or a where, you must accept it; rejecting it is creative blocking. Even if the rejection gets you a laugh, your partner will feel frustrated and the improvisation will lose energy and die at that point. For instance, if your partner says, "It's so comfortable sitting on this beach with you because we've known each other so long," you may say, "I hate the beach, it's full of sand fleas" without negating the who, what or where.

In fact, contrasts and opposites ("so comfortable"/"I hate") are the stuff of theatre and always make a scene interesting. You may not say, "What do you mean we've known each other so long. We've just met" or "You're not sitting, you're standing on your head" or "Beach? This is a cumulus cloud." Any of those would be creative blocking. The only way to make an improvisation work is to work together.

The games I describe here are a few selected from many. In my experience, these few are most useful during rehearsals for a play and in this workshop are best done in the order I have presented them, from least threatening onward.

Once you are in rehearsal, having done the workshop, you, as director, will be able to call out—"stage picture" or "creative blocking" so that the players can respond without stopping the play. Individual "offenders" are not singled out. Everyone in the group can benefit from the directive.

As you are explaining each game to the actors, include the game's purpose.

FORTUNATELY/UNFORTUNATELY
PURPOSE:
To become conscious of the effects of positive and negative response on ourselves and others.

HOW TO PLAY:

Have each person choose a partner and call herself A or B. A starts a statement that begins with "fortunately." B continues the story with "unfortunately." For example:

> **A:** Fortunately, I won a lottery.
> **B:** Unfortunately, I lost the ticket.
> **A:** Fortunately, my cousin found it on the dashboard of the car.
> **B:** Unfortunately, I rolled down the window and it blew away.
> **A:** Fortunately, a bird caught the ticket in its beak.
> **B:** Unfortunately, the bird did not stop flying.

As a group, reflect on how it felt to be A and how it felt to be B.
A and B then switch roles, play the game again, and follow-up with a reflection.

RENAMING

PURPOSE:

To begin to break down our tendency to edit our thoughts and to learn to accept the first thing that comes into our minds.

HOW TO PLAY:

Have the whole group move around the room and as rapidly as possible, point to familiar objects and name each one with the first thing that comes to mind. For example, point to a window and say, "rug" to a chair and say, "shoe" and so on. Everyone does this simultaneously pointing very deliberately and shouting out the names that come first to their minds. This is a good drama warm-up because it involves everyone in large action and no one is in the "spotlight." It is also wonderfully chaotic and much more difficult to do than it seems.

EXPLOSION TAG

PURPOSE:

To get the body and voice into full action, to make physical contact with one another, and to shake out the inhibitions.

HOW TO PLAY:

Find an open, uncluttered space and begin with a brief game of regular tag played within boundaries. Then the leader (you) will clap twice and whoever is "it" remains "it," but everyone moves in slow motion. The leader then claps twice once more and again who ever is "it" at the moment remains "it" and everyone goes back to regular speed. This time, however, when each person is tagged, he or she becomes "it" as usual, but also must explode. There is no set way to explode. Explosion is a spontaneous action and/or sound at the moment of being tagged and is continued by each player until everyone is tagged or exhaustion has set in, whichever comes first. This, too, is a good drama warm-up.

DIE

PURPOSE:

To improve concentration, clean up language skills, and develop impromptu speech and movement abilities.

HOW TO PLAY:

Ask five or six players to sit in a straight line, not too close to one another, facing the audience. The audience is you and the rest of the group and if the total group is small the audience is you alone. In improvisation, the audience (never the players themselves) must tell the players who they are and where they are. In this game, all of the players are one person. The who is always a type of person, not a specific person (a nurse, a rock singer, not Florence Nightingale or Madonna) and the where needs to be a place the players can visualize, not simply geographical (the woods, not British Columbia). For a creative start, the who and the where should not be a logical combination such as teacher in a classroom. Better to put her in a circus ring or in a tree house.

A game director is chosen from the audience group and he or she begins the game by pointing to one of the players (game director's choice) who starts telling a story as the audience-designated who (a rock singer, for instance) in the designated where (a closet). As soon as the game director points to another player the previous speaker must stop and the new player picks up the story mid-sentence without stammering, hesitation, or repeating words. When a player causes the story to lapse or keeps it from continuing smoothly, the audience shouts "die!" The "offending" player then steps into the area between players and audience, immediately names a place and a weapon (a where and a what) and dramatically enacts his or her death. She then joins the audience and an audience member takes her place as a player and someone else becomes game director. Or if only half the group have been players, switch groups; audience become players, players become audience.

GIBBERISH

PURPOSE:

To show how we communicate through body language and sound, and to help actors move away from an exclusive reliance on words. A good game to play during rehearsal when an actor sounds "wooden."

HOW TO PLAY:

Have four to eight players sit in a circle, on the floor if possible, give them a who and a where, for example, a convention of dentists in the woods. Then ask them to hold a conversation using no known language, simply gibberish sounds they invent. Babies routinely express a range of emotions and thought by babbling a variety of sounds. Demonstrate some gibberish to them to help them feel more comfortable doing it themselves. They should have real thoughts in their heads as they speak gibberish and they should attempt to draw everyone into the conversation. Then when the spirit moves, one of the players must "take stage" (become the focus) and urgently try to get the group, as a whole, to do something. The other players have to co-operate if the one who has taken stage can communicate the urgent task.

This ends the game. Give them feedback on what you saw communicated and how it did or didn't come together into one scene.

STAGE PICTURE
PURPOSE:

To help actors explore the use of space, to learn to give and take stage, and to develop skills for impromptu dialogue. This game can be a warm-up when using the whole cast, and is very useful in blocking visually interesting crowd scenes and bringing them to life. Stage Picture is a versatile game from which you can even develop entire original scripts.

HOW TO PLAY:

Divide a large group in half. One half of the group stands in the playing area as the players and the others sit facing them as the audience. Direct the players to move in and around and between one another, making eye contact with each other as they pass. Eye contact is the starting point of relationship and whole-body movement keeps our imaginations flowing. Continue to direct them to keep moving and keep making eye contact. Then call out "stage picture." This is not a freeze, but rather an opportunity for the players to choose a spot to be in and to take a pose in relation to someone else or the space and to hold it. They might be lying down, reaching up high, or posed anywhere in the middle. Next, ask the audience to tell the players if there is anyone whom they cannot see a comfortable amount of. The players then adjust their positions for sight according to the directions from the audience remembering that it is the blocked person who must move not the blocker. Actors soon learn that if they choose to take a low position they have to be in the front and if there is an actor directly in front of them they need to move out from behind that actor.

In rehearsal you may do only this much if you wish to arrange a crowd scene, but if you want them to develop characters through improvisation continue with the rest of this game.

Ask the audience group to imagine what has just happened that resulted in this picture. For example, a bomb has just exploded, Suzie in the middle has just jumped off the roof, or the show has just ended. This is the what. And who are they as a group? Are they a corps de ballet, a bunch of school children, or a collection of strangers? The audience may want to name some relationships between characters to give the actors more to work with. And where are they? In this game the audience may name a logical place if they wish.

Then, as director, ask the players to speak and act to bring the scene alive based on the information they have been given. When you think they have got something out of this and before the energy runs out, call an end to the scene. You and the audience now give feedback. Look particularly for someone who "took the stage" effectively and others who gave it by listening and responding. A group of actors will tend to divide themselves into pairs or trios and begin to develop competing scenes simultaneously. They will need to learn to listen and watch for a focus and contribute to it so that all the players are creating just one scene together. Remember always, in giving feedback, to insist that the group, starting with the players themselves, comment on the specific, positive aspects first, then give constructive criticism. The essence of creativity is to see beauty first.

Finally, switch groups and do it all again.

Basic Acting Tips to Share at Rehearsals

MEMORIZING LINES AND CUES

Until they gain a fair amount of experience, actors will be nervous about learning and remembering lines. They need to understand that the real work of developing characters and bringing a play to life can only begin *after* the lines are learned. They might need to be reminded that it is just as important to learn the cues for the lines so that they know when to say them.

It is good at the first rehearsal, after the workshop, to take them through the blocking so that they can envision themselves in motion while they are learning their lines and cues for the second rehearsal.

Short simple dramas may only need two rehearsals and people with very few lines can learn them during rehearsal. As to the main fear, that of forgetting the lines (adults fear this much more than children) remind them that the lines are really not sacrosanct. The Bible has many translations and so can a script, as long as the cues are still recognizable. This fear of forgetting can also provide additional motivation for deep breathing. The added oxygen really does feed the brain and the deep breathing does relax tensions and helps to remove physical, emotional, intellectual, and spiritual blocks. Memorization is ideal but, if not accomplished, improvisation will be fun and will keep the drama alive.

For longer dramas the following points may be helpful when memorizing lines:

- The actor should first "memorize" the thought progression of each scene before memorizing the actual lines. For example,

    1. Greet Mrs. Brown.
    2. Tell her you need more time.
    3. Insist on being heard.
    4. Listen to her arguments.
    5. Leave angrily.

Memory work needs always to include scenes as whole units, not isolated lines or speeches.

- Memorize cues as well as lines. Again, it is more important to know what is happening rather than what is being said.

- Break down each section of a scene into individual beats or sub-sections, giving each a title with a central core verb appropriate to the actor (for instance, "Making a Phone Call" or "Arriving in Jerusalem"). This will also help the actor memorize the thought progression of the scene.

- Try memorizing lines without putting emotion or interpretation behind them, much as we learn the vocabulary of a foreign language. This will help to avoid rehearsing incorrect interpretations that will have to be unlearned later. It is easier to memorize this way than it is to unlearn what you have memorized.

- Memorize lines in a short amount of time. Set deadlines and keep them. Long rehearsal periods where some actors continue to need their scripts results in a very uneven finished product and large gaps in character development.

- Consider devoting one or two rehearsals to allow actors to run scenes straight through for the sole purpose of memorizing. This may prove to be the wisest use of time.

DIRECTIONS

These directions are indicated in all scripts and are used in communication between directors and actors.

- Up stage refers to the back of the stage (or chancel). It was once common for stages to be raked (slanted downward from back to front).

- Down stage is closest to the audience.

- Centre stage is in the centre.

- Right and left stage are from the actor's point of view when facing the audience.

An important rule to maintain is that actors move *only* on their own lines not on anyone else's, this includes standing up and sitting down, as well as moving from point A to point B.

ENTRANCES AND EXITS

- Off stage space: It is important for the actors to know where they are coming from when they enter and where they are going when they exit, within the context of the play. Knowing the who, what, where is necessary in script work as well as in improvisation. They know the play is set in a kitchen but what room are they coming from and what room are they exiting to? The same is needed for exterior scenes, of course. There may be indication in the script for this but, often, it is simply your choice.

- Moment Before: Non-professional actors frequently want to go over their lines in their heads before they go on. It would be far better for them to spend sixty seconds getting into character by living through, in their minds and in detail, the moment in the character's life before the character steps out onto the stage. The actor must make the moment logical for the character and the situation but, with a creative imagination, that moment will be rich in detail and the actor will step on stage fully in character.

- Endings: When dramas, and scenes within dramas, end with actors on stage, have them remain still for three beats before exiting. Remember the drama is not over until all actors are out of sight or have returned to their pews, so encourage them to stay in character.

HIGH STATUS/LOW STATUS

This is a way of developing character from the outside in. The character who has high status in a scene is the one who is in control. In a short drama emperors or other powerful characters may play in high status throughout the play. Sometimes a character may be in high status one moment then be made to feel vulnerable and go into low status the next. A meek or gentle character usually plays in low status.

To achieve high status from the outside in, stand or sit erect and absolutely still. Do not move your head. You will find that, when you speak, your voice and delivery will be affected by your body and pose and you will be performing in high status. Conversely, if you squirm, wiggle or nod your feet, arms, hands and, particularly, your head you will come across with vulnerability and you will speak and act in low status. Try it! (You as the director may need the high-status trick.) Once the actors are aware of this technique you can call out high status or low status during rehearsal when you feel the need.

NARRATION AND READING

If there is a narrator he or she will be the one who holds the drama together during the performance. Narrator scripts should be enlarged for easy visibility and they need to mark their scripts during rehearsal. Marking for pauses is particularly important as this includes pausing for the action and the lines of the actors. The narrator needs to keep one eye on the script and one eye on the actors to cover for any difficulties, but never to prompt. It is much better for the drama for the actors and/or narrator to use improvisation, until all are back on track, rather than to prompt.

When reading, nouns and verbs are stressed as they carry the subject and action of the play. Descriptive words tend to come across through inflection and body language. Perhaps the most important skill in reading is eye contact, not the head-bobbing-up-and-down sort but real eye contact. With practice you can learn to read one line out loud while reading the next line in your head, remembering that next line just long enough to share it with the audience. By running your finger down the margin of the text while you are reading, you will be able to keep your place so that you can hold eye contact for the entire line before returning to the text. When preparing your text you will want to underline the lines and phrases that you particularly want to share with full eye contact. A good way to practise this regularly is while singing hymns. Read one line, look around at the congregation for the next. No one will ever know you've been practising eye contact on Sunday mornings.

Physical Stuff

This book is not about elaborate costumes, sets or props, because I feel there are simpler and more effective ways to smoothly move drama in and out of a service of worship or a meeting.

FABRIC AS SET AND EFFECT

Long lengths of lining or synthetic silk fabric (twelve feet and more) can represent anything from a tent to the elements or the breath of God depending on how it is handled. Of course, their expensive cousins, real silk and gold or silver lamé work very well too. Coat and dress lining comes in a variety of colours but if you are anywhere near a shop that sells "silk" blend fabric for making saris go there.

Put one person on either end of a long piece of fabric in a large room or church aisle and give them some time to experiment with moving it through the air. Use several pieces of fabric with several pairs of people and they will discover what the fabric will do through experimenting with it. People have brought amazing life to long widths of blue, green, silver, and yellow fabric while the story of Genesis was read, giving visual form to the creation story. Long widths of bright red have provided the parting of the Red Sea and on another occasion this red fabric represented the cross as it was carried over the actor's shoulder and trailed behind him as he walked up the centre aisle. The fabric fills the often high ceiling and long aisles of a church marvelously with colour and symbolism, and it is easily portable. For greater control of the fabric, sew a hem on each end of the length of fabric and slip a length of dowel (available at hardware stores) into the hems.

SPACE AND LEVELS

Placing the players on different levels is essential for visual interest. You can make good use of your church's architecture for levels and for set pieces. Often the pulpit is a natural place for an emperor or other "high status" character to stand and balconies are useful for whole scenes that need distance from the main action.

High stools are quite useful as they lift a seated player up for visibility and are easy to bring on and remove during a service. If you have narrators, they need to be visible and they need to be able to see the other players, as the narration both guides and follows the action but should not upstage the action. Placing music stands for the script and high stools on the nave floor works well for narrators and for whole staged readings.

For additional levels, simple folding platforms can be made. I've found that a collection of the sturdy plastic milk boxes available for a dollar or two from grocery stores can be useful. The actors can each bring one on stage and use them individually or pushed together to make a platform for one or more to sit or stand on.

And do make symbolic use of the elements of the church that are always there. A congregation can gain an enriched understanding of communion or baptism if you give the altar or font a symbolic significance in your drama.

COSTUMES

If you are working with children and doing a biblical pageant everyone may be disappointed if it is not fully costumed. Otherwise, however, for liturgical drama I prefer simplicity and symbolism, such as using colour to delineate groups of characters either with the whole costume or with a bland colour outfit and a designated colour accent (hat, scarf, sash); for instance, have the good guys all wear yellow, their adversaries, red and the surrounding crowds, blue. The traditional church rummage sale or bazaar is an ideal supplier for hats and costume pieces. Usually, what you most want for drama, the general public doesn't want at all.

MASKS

One more item of costume that is particularly effective with mime is the mask. One can purchase masks or make them from a variety of materials. I will describe the plaster bandage style because the process of making it develops relationships and trust and is wonderfully messy. Neatness and creativity are not often companions.

I recommend this process for adults and older children, nine years and older.

YOU WILL NEED:

- large bowls or pots filled with warm water
- scissors
- containers of vaseline
- a roll of medium width plaster bandage per mask (this can be purchased at a surgical supply store by the roll or by the box). If you have trouble finding this ask your local hospital where they buy theirs.
- talcum powder for a finishing touch is optional
- towels for individual cover-up and clean-up
- large-eye darning needles and fine elastic

PROCEDURE:

1. Choose or prepare an environment that can be cleaned up easily afterward. Divide the mask makers into pairs, A to sit at a table and B to create the mask on A.

2. A puts on protective clothing and pins all hair back from the face. B fills a large pot with warm water (two sets of pairs can use the same large pot) and begins to cut a roll of bandages into strips 7 to 10 cm (3 to 4 inches) long. Be sure to cut very narrow strips for the small areas, like between the nostrils. It is helpful to have an extra person or persons to move around cutting strips for the mask makers.

3. B covers every inch of A's face with vaseline, including the sensitive area around the eyes, just below the jawline, the hairline itself, eyebrows, mustache, and beard. Any area where the plaster bandage is applied that is not covered with vaseline will hurt when the mask is removed.

4. B quickly dips a bandage strip into the pot, squeezes out excess water, also quickly, and smoothes the strip onto A's face. Cover the entire face with one layer then go around again with a second layer. Add a third layer for a stronger mask, particularly at the temples where the elastic will be attached. Always work around the eyes leaving eye holes. You may also leave the mouth uncovered or not as you wish, or make a half-mask covering the face to just below the nose and cheek bones.

5. When complete, the masks are ready to remove in minutes. B gently wiggles the mask off A.

6. Immediately and liberally sprinkle talcum powder over the surface of the mask, gently rubbing it in with finger tips for a slightly glossy finish.

7. Very carefully (the masks are delicate until they are fully dry) drive a hole with the needle through each temple for later attachment of elastic.

8. Then B places it where it can dry for a minimum of twenty-four hours without being disturbed.

9. A can clean up and carry out the same procedure for B.

In a day or two, when the masks are dry, their wearers will need to wipe off excess vaseline from the inside, trim them for comfort and appearance, and attach a fine elastic through the holes at the temples.

These masks are very personal and will only really fit the one on whom they were made. This type of mask, white and without character embellishment, is known as a universal mask. Actors should be encouraged to treat them with great respect, as an extension of themselves, and as a symbol of the common humanity in all of us.

Whole-face masks are worn exclusively in mime and can help an actor develop expressive bodies, the ability to play in heroic dimensions, simplicity, and economy in movement. In rehearsal, once a scene is stopped and the actors must talk, the mask is slipped to the top of the head and worn there for the necessary time. When the mask is on the face, it is best to avoid touching it, miming, eating or drinking. The mask loses its conviction when it is confronted directly with its inability to move. Use half-masks, if you want the wearers to speak, etc.

MASK WORK

Masks can offer everyone a certain self-knowledge, through a false face one can find a true face. As a sensitive actor, approach a mask first by simply looking at it; here the identification begins. Then put the mask on and remain still. Empty your mind of plans and your body of customary rhythms and movements. Even empty your lungs of air so that something different can come to you with a fresh breath. Observe yourself in a mirror, letting the identification pervade your body, then gradually search for the appropriate posture, walk, and small gestures. A fusion of person and mask takes place that brings the Latin word *persona* (mask) full circle. When that fusion is achieved, you will feel a sense of simplicity plus authority. You can "carry" the mask.

The mask calls for movement larger than life, more important than minor or trivial actions. One can not simply don a mask and go about one's ordinary business.

SOME MASK EXERCISES

- Move through everyday activities—dressing, working, preparing food. Aim to do them simply, with no unnecessary movements.

- Move like animals, elements, objects. Find the form, the rhythm, and the movement of each identification.

- Act out the cycle of elements—water is evaporated by sun that is hidden by clouds that are dispersed by wind that is stopped by mountains that are eroded by water.

You may, of course also use these masks to create a larger than life individual character in contrast to the universal mask. Determine the dominate characteristic of your character and trim the mouth and eye openings into a set expression adding bold, black life-lines to the face.

On assuming a character mask, actors often try immediately to be the character. Some movements may be effective but, as in the previous exercises, the mask should be given time to do its work. It is better to refrain from quickly imposing gesture on the mask; let the mask transform the image in the actor's imagination into movement in its own time. The restraint will also help the actor to do what may at first seem like too little, for the mask amplifies everything that touches upon it. If the actor does less, the mask does more.

If your players perform together frequently, mask making and voice and theatre game sessions held on a regular basis are enormously beneficial and fun.

The drama depends upon your concept for it and your creative imagination as you read the text and as you work with the players. In addition to presenting stories to your congregation in new and exciting ways, doing drama has the added benefit of establishing meaningful relationships among the players. Always allow them time to get to know one another and to enjoy the experience.

Glossary of Theatre Terms

Beats—subsections of a scene in a script that are connected in thought or action

Blocked—when an actor allows her- or himself to be obscured from the audience's view while on stage

Blocking—the broad physical movements of the characters on stage as well as their entrances and exits

Centre Stage—the centre of the stage

Creative Blocking—negating another actor's established Who, What, or Where (not allowed in improvisation)

Cues—the final words of another actor's lines that precede your lines

Down Stage—the stage area closest to the audience

Drama Warm-up—a process that involves everyone in large action in relationship with one-another with no one in the "spotlight"

Give Stage—to release the focus and allow another actor to take stage

High Status—a character played in stillness as commanding and coolly powerful

Improvisation—unscripted drama based on a Who, What, and Where

Levels—different heights of playing areas on the stage

Lines—the sentences an actor speaks

Low Status—a character played with much movement as warm, vulnerable, and powerless

Stage Picture—actors in interesting groupings and poses

Stage Right and Stage Left—determined by the actor's right and left when facing the audience

Take Stage—to allow your character to become the focus on stage

To Up-stage (verb)—to position yourself up stage of another actor thereby forcing him or her to turn his or her back to the audience to speak to you (a practice generally frowned upon)

Up Stage—the stage area farthest from the audience

Spring

Spring like youth's passion
births hope and play and laughter
to revive our souls

Can We Be with Her, Too?

Carolyn Pogue

Reflection in worship or at a meeting
This could be preceded by a reading of Matthew 27:1–5
Performance time: 2 to 3 minutes

CHARACTERS:
Woman
Second Voice for prayer

TREATMENT AND SETTING:
Performed as a monologue as indicated in the script or as a dramatic reading from the front.

— ◆ —

(Woman in historical or everyday dress rushes into the back of the sanctuary. She is breathless. Loud. She addresses the congregation directly.)

You're here! Thanks be to God! I need you. She needs you!

(Moves forward up the aisle.)

We were there when they told her what he'd done!

(Quieter)

You should have seen her.
Do you know what it's like to see a heart shatter? Have you seen it?
She stood still when they told her. Stock still!

(Moves to the front of the sanctuary.)

She turned pale. Her eyes went big.
She bowed her head a moment, then raised it towards heaven, and a sound came from her. It was an ancient sound, like an animal.
Like the sound of trees in a storm.
Like a rock splitting!

(Pause)

Then she seemed to shrink before my eyes.
No one touched her or held her or stood near her.
No one could believe that such a thing could happen
to a friend —
like you. Or me.
It was bad enough. Dreadful enough. Shameful enough.
And then they told her the rest.
That her boy was dead.
He killed himself, they said.
And what was left of her,
What was left of that mother-woman
Seemed to disappear before my eyes...

> *(She is seeing this again in her mind's eye. Urgently.)*

We have to help her!
We've been friends all our lives—

laughed and cried and complained together
cooked and sewed and shopped together
been at each other's weddings
buried our parents
raised our kids...

> *(Pause)*

Can we be with her now
in this shameful time,
this sad, terrifying time?
Can we be with the mother of Judas?

> *(The woman freezes in place, and then another voice speaks.)*

Creator God, our mother and our father,
You weep with us when we weep our confusion and sorrow.
You laugh with us when we laugh our joy.

Today we remember the humanity of your child, Jesus. We remember the humanity of his friends and their families.

We remember our human connection to their laughter and their tears. Give us the courage to walk with the bereaved, the shamed, the joyless ones.

Give us tender hearts to stand with those who feel despised. In the name of Jesus, who calls us to compassion for all that is living.

Amen.

A Holy Week Broadcast

David Kai

Scripture and sermon for Palm/Passion Sunday, Maundy Thursday, or
Good Friday
Performance time: 25 to 30 minutes

CHARACTERS:
SPEAKING ROLES:
Eva-reporter—a bit haughty
Adam-reporter—earnest, average
Jerry Myah-anchor person—fond of sensationalism and ratings

NON-SPEAKING ROLES:
The Corps-twelve (more or less) actors to play multi-character parts—
     Jesus, crowd, disciples, women at the tomb

TREATMENT:
Some hymns are suggested, but other appropriate hymns/music could be
substituted.
   The play could be done entirely in modern dress or entirely in biblical
dress or the three reporters could wear modern dress and the corps, biblical dress. The corps in this drama could be played by people with no experience in acting, so you might take the opportunity to invite people who
have never participated in the liturgy in this way before to try it. Eva,
Adam, and Jerry could memorize their lines for a full dramatic performance or they could read the text from music stands at one side of the action. If they are reading they should be very familiar with the script and
use good reading technique.

SETTING:
Eva and Adam wear prop earphones and carry microphones (working ones, if
possible). They will rove about in the biblical scene, probably best located in
the chancel as the play's focus. Jerry has a microphone and prop mixing con-
sole and could have a JOB RADIO sign. He is located in a separate area, this
could be at a table at one side of the chancel or in the pulpit or in a balcony (if
he is visible). He could also be in a pew in the midst of the congregation.

SCENE ONE

The Streets Of Jerusalem

ADAM:	*(Speaking into mike.)* Check one! Check two! Do we have a signal? Okay, great. *(To Eva)* We'll be on the air in about 30 seconds.
EVA:	Thirty seconds until the end of my career. I don't know why I was ever put on this assignment. After all, I'm supposed to be the fashion reporter.
ADAM:	Why not just be happy that you have a job? These are tough times, you know.
EVA:	*(Haughty)* Of course, why should I expect a hayseed like you to understand. This is really quite below me— tramping around on these dusty old back roads when I should be by the runways of Rome…
ADAM:	*(Listening to earphone.)* You'd better stop complaining and get ready. The station is buzzing us now.
EVA:	…and it might be at least tolerable if the company were a bit more interesting…
JERRY:	Okay, get ready—we're on the air in 5, 4, 3, 2….*(clicks switch)* We're back! And that was "Bim bom," the latest number one single from the Qumran Quartet. And you're listening to Jerusalem Official Broadcasting; J-O-B Radio—the station with the patience to wait for that late-breaking news story. I'm your host, Jerry Myah, bringing you all the latest and greatest happenings from the holy city. Today there's been quite a commotion by the main gates; here with an update are our roving reporters, Adam and Eva.

ADAM:	Thanks, Jerry. We're standing above the main gates where the crowds are literally falling over each other. As we speak, a huge procession is passing by this spot, led by the popular prophet, Jesus of Nazareth. The enormous crowd is ecstatic. They are waving palm branches and laying their coats in his path. I'm sure that you can hear the crowd shouting.
THE CORPS:	Hosanna! Blessed is the one who comes in the name of the Lord! (*As they move up the centre aisle making the path smooth for Jesus who mimes riding a donkey.*)
JERRY:	Eva, could you describe this Jesus for those who have never seen him in person? What does he look like? What is he wearing?
EVA:	Well, Jerry, in my opinion he looks quite ordinary; he is definitely underdressed for this kind of occasion. In fact, I doubt that he is wearing anything other than his regular street clothes—which may be making a statement in itself. But this is obviously a very low-budget affair. He's even riding a humble donkey—and a borrowed one at that! Not very impressive, if you ask me—anyone of real importance would be riding something more stylish—horses and chariots at least.
ADAM:	Now let's not be too hasty in our judgements here. After all, this is someone that a lot of people are calling the Messiah—even the Son of God!
EVA:	Just another wild-eyed prophet with an attitude, if you ask me. And his followers—even worse! Mostly scruffy fishing people from the outlying provinces.
ADAM:	And yet there are many, even among our own religious leaders who think that this Jesus does have an authentic message from God.

EVA: So, Adam, why don't you just quit your job and become one of his fanatical followers?

ADAM: Shh—we're still on the air, you know.

EVA: Trust me, Adam—this Jesus fellow will be forgotten by next week. As soon as things get tough, he'll be gone just like all the rest of them.

JERRY: Okay, you two. Stop arguing and just stick to the facts. We'll get back to you later for any further developments.

EVA: All right, Jerry. This is Eva…

ADAM: …and Adam…

EVA and ADAM: …reporting for JOB News.

JERRY: And now, back to more music on JOB Radio.

> *(Hymn: "Hosanna, Loud Hosanna" or other appropriate hymn.)*
>
> *(The Corps exit during hymn.)*

SCENE TWO

The Upper Room

(Twelve of the Corps enter, each with a chair, and sit around the altar or other table in the centre of the chancel, one person brings two chairs so that there is an empty one. Freeze in a variety of eating positions or each slowly mime eating without talking.)

JERRY: We're back, folks. And wasn't that a fine selection from Junior Choir and the All-stars? I see that we have another update from our roving reporters, Adam and Eva. Come in, Adam and Eva. Where are you now?

ADAM: We're here at the Upper Room in downtown Jerusalem where Jesus is now sharing a meal with the disciples.

EVA: It looks as if all the disciples are here—except for the one named Judas Iscariot. He made a hasty exit a few minutes ago; perhaps he needs to buy some more provisions for the meal.

JERRY: And can you tell us what kind of meal this is?

ADAM: Well, at this point it appears to consist mostly of bread and wine.

EVA: Bread and wine—that's pretty common fare for such supposed royalty, don't you think?

ADAM: Perhaps; but I think the important part was the meaning that he gave to that simple food. Jesus took the bread, blessed it and broke it, and gave it to the disciples and said "This is my body, broken for you." And then he took a cup of wine, blessed it, gave it to the disciples and said, "This is my blood, shed for you."

JERRY: It sounds as if Jesus expects something terrible to happen to him.

36

EVA: Well, it wouldn't surprise me at all. The talk around town is that the chief priests and scribes are looking for an excuse to arrest him.

ADAM: And it seems clear to me from his words that Jesus is willing to sacrifice himself for his friends.

EVA: After the meal, Jesus and the disciples will be going to the Garden of Gethsemane to pray. We'll be following them, and we'll be back with an update in a little while. Until that time, this is Eva…

ADAM: …and Adam…

EVA and ADAM: …signing off for JOB News.

> *(Hymn: "An Upper Room" or "We Hail Thee Now" or another appropriate hymn.)*

> *(The Corps exit with their chairs. Jesus and some of the disciples return immediately to assemble in small stage picture groups, some in prayer, some asleep during the hymn. When the hymn ends the other half of the corps runs on threateningly. They enact the Judas kiss and take Jesus away. The others exit running off the other way.)*

SCENE THREE

The Garden of Gethsemane

JERRY:	You're listening to JOB Radio. And we take you now to the Garden of Gethsemane where some dramatic developments have taken place in the continuing saga of Jesus of Nazareth. Come in please, Adam and Eva….
EVA:	We're standing in the garden where only a few minutes ago, Jesus and his disciples were surprised by an angry mob led by the disciple, Judas Iscariot. Or perhaps I should say, former disciple, since he has obviously become a traitor to his old cause. The mob came here to arrest Jesus and bring him before the high priest.
JERRY:	And what was Jesus' reaction to all of this?
ADAM:	Jerry, Jesus was remarkably calm. He told his disciples not to fight—he didn't want any casualties. Then he told the mob to leave the disciples alone, because it was only he that they wanted. At that point the disciples ran and were able to escape. So Jesus literally sacrificed himself for his followers.
EVA:	I hate to admit it, Jerry, but even I was impressed. There seems to be more to this Jesus character than I had given him credit for.
JERRY:	So where does the story go from here?
ADAM:	Jesus will be taken to the high priest to face charges of blasphemy; from there, he'll likely be brought before Pilate for sentencing, probably some time in the morning.
EVA:	We'll be in touch as soon as there are some new developments.

JERRY: Thanks, Adam and Eva. Bye for now.

EVA and ADAM: Goodbye.

JERRY: We'll be sure to follow this story closely and bring you all the exciting details. So keep your dial tuned and your ears glued to JOB Radio—the station with the patience to wait for that late-breaking news story. This ends our broadcast day, but we'll be back as soon as the rooster crows. Good night, and shalom.

> *(Hymn: "Go to Dark Gethsemane" or other appropriate hymn.)*

> *(Adam and Eva are off stage at one microphone. Jerry is in his usual place.)*

SCENE FOUR

At the cross

JERRY:	Good morning, and welcome back to JOB Radio. We interrupt our regular programming to bring you a special report from our roving reporters. Good morning, Adam and Eva, are you there?
ADAM:	*(Serious)* Yes, we're here—but one could hardly call it a good morning. We're standing on the hill just outside Jerusalem called Golgotha, or Skull Hill, the site where executions are typically carried out.
EVA:	Earlier this morning, Jesus was sentenced to death by Pilate, who incidentally, could find no fault in him. However, rumours that Jesus had proclaimed himself to be some kind of royalty were used to accuse him of treason against Rome. After the sentencing, Jesus was beaten terribly by the guards. Mockingly, a crown of thorns was placed on his head, and he was forced to carry his own cross. On the way to Golgotha, Jesus collapsed, and a passerby was forced to help him with the cross.

> *(Nailing sound begins—Eva continues to speak, but more and more hesitantly and quietly.)*

	Now Jesus is being nailed to—to the cross—and—*(voice breaking)* I'm sorry—Adam, take over. *(Nailing ends.)*
JERRY:	Eva, we can't hear you. What's going on now? Eva? Adam?
ADAM:	*(Slowly)* Adam here.
JERRY:	Adam, what's happening there? *(Pause)* Adam?
ADAM:	*(Slowly)* I—I can't believe it—but Jesus is actually asking God to forgive the ones who put him on the cross.

JERRY: Yes, yes, but tell us more; we can't have all this dead air time, you know.

ADAM: *(Pause)* Oh, have some respect, Jerry, at least this once.

JERRY: What are you talking about? Our audience wants to know what's going on! And for that matter, so do I!

ADAM: No, it's not necessary. This is Adam, signing off for JOB News.

JERRY: Signing off?! You can't sign off now! Adam?! *(Flicking switch.)* Excuse me folks—we seem to be experiencing some technical difficulties. We'll be right back after this commercial message….*(flicking switch)* Adam! Eva! I know you can hear me! Don't mess with me; I'm warning you! I won't have this shoddy excuse for reporting! Remember—your jobs are in my hands! Not necessary, eh? We'll see what is and isn't necessary at your performance reviews.

               (Hymn: "Beneath the Cross of Jesus" or other appropriate hymn.)

SCENE FIVE

At the tomb

> *(As hymn ends, two or three women enter and kneel outside the closed tomb—this can be a tomb set piece or it might be something symbolic such as a communion rail, a cross or an appropriate stain glass window. Make sure that the kneeling actors are visible to the congregation. Jerry is still in place; Adam and Eva enter from the side.)*

JERRY: You're listening to JOB Radio. Folks, we seem to have overcome our technical difficulties, and once again, here are our roving reporters, Adam and Eva.

ADAM: We're standing in a garden owned by Joseph of Arimathea, where Jesus' body was brought after his death. His body has been placed in a tomb hewn from a rocky outcropping, and a large stone has been rolled in front of its entrance.

EVA: Some of Jesus' followers are here, praying outside the tomb. It is a very moving scene to witness their dedication to Jesus, even in death. It is obvious that Jesus meant *(slowing down)* a great deal to many people, and—in—fact…

> *(Eva pauses for a moment, puts down microphone, walks slowly over to those kneeling by the tomb and kneels beside them.)*

JERRY: Eva? Now where has she gone? Adam?—Are you still there?—Can you tell us more? —Can you get an interview with someone? *(Adam also puts down mike, kneels beside others at the tomb.)* Answer me, will you? *(Flicks switch, pauses.)* Folks, we seem to have been cut off— and Adam and Eva, if you can hear me, consider yourselves cut off too! *(Pause—then speaks slowly and reflec-*

tively.) You know folks, some people have their priorities all mixed up; I mean, what can be so important about this Jesus fellow? Two or two thousand years from now, who's going to remember anything about him? Anyway, this is Jerry Myah, signing off for JOB Radio. Good-bye and shalom.

(People by tomb remain until end of service. Jerry exits during hymn.)

— ◆ —

The service might conclude with prayers for the Family of God, and the singing of "Were You There When They Crucified My Lord?"

The Tables Turned and the Stone Gets Rolled Away

Scott Douglas

Scripture and sermon based on John 20:11–18
Performance time: 25 minutes

CHARACTERS:

Mary—a woman in her late twenties, possibly with a history of mental illness. She is a follower of Jesus.

Micah—a man of indeterminate age. He has been unemployed for more than eight years.

Esther—a woman in her seventies who lives in poverty.

OR FOR LARGER CAST VERSION:

Mary
Micah
Esther
Jesus
Money Changer
Crowd of Poor
High Priest

TREATMENT:

This play is very effective as:

1. A fully staged and, of course, memorized play with a cast of three as indicated in the script. This would be the most powerful method of staging this play.

2. A staged reading with stools and podiums in the centre of the chancel with Micah on stage right, Mary in the middle, and Esther on stage left. Include the change of hats for a reading.

3. A larger cast version is with Jesus, Money Changer and High Priest as separate characters and you could also include a crowd of the poor. For this I suggest modern dress for Micah, Mary, and Esther and biblical garb for Jesus, Money Changer, and High Priest. I would suggest dressing the crowd of poor as street people of today.

SETTING:

Divide the playing space into two areas—one for the tomb and one for the temple. The tomb could be designated by pots of flowers or simply an open space with a bench in it. For treatment 1 the temple area would have a folding table and coins near by for Micah to set up. For treatment 3 the table could already be set up in the temple area.

For all versions you will need; a strip of white cloth, a large paper shopping bag, a visor cap, an impressive looking hat—a folding table—a variety of coins, and a bench.

The scene takes place outside an empty tomb.

— ◆ —

> *(Mary is sitting outside the tomb, weeping. In her arms she holds a balled-up strip of white linen. Micah and Esther approach her. Esther is carrying a large paper shopping bag. Micah taps Mary on the shoulder.)*

MICAH: Hey Mary, what are you crying about?

> *(Mary is surprised and quickly backs away from them.)*

ESTHER: Oh, now, you see? I told you you'd startle her. *(To Mary)* It's all right, dear. We're friends.

MARY: I'm sorry, do I know you?

ESTHER: Perhaps not, dear. But we know you.

MICAH: Your friends left hours ago. What are you still doing here?

MARY: I don't know. Waiting, I guess?

MICAH: Waiting for what?

> *(Pause)*

MARY: …I don't know.

ESTHER: (*Sympathetically*) It's been a hard couple of days for you, hasn't it?

MARY: They stole his body, you know. As if it wasn't enough, they had to steal his body too.

ESTHER: Indeed. It certainly looks that way.

MARY: It would have been better if I'd never met him. He should have just left me possessed by demons, out of control, without a voice of my own. I mean, what's the use of being shown a world of freedom when, in the end, nothing changes. The poor are still poor. The evil are still evil. And death has the last word. None of it mattered.

(Micah sits down beside Mary.)

MICAH: I know what you mean. I used to feel that way too. No money, no job, no family, no nothing. I'd had enough of it all, so I just went blind. I filled my eyes with fog so I wouldn't have to look at the world around me, and I hid myself away in dark corners. But then one day I realized, hey, if nobody sees me then nobody knows there's a problem. Everyone goes on as if everything's fine. So I dragged and stumbled my way to the Temple, 'cause, even though I didn't want to see, I did want to be seen. That way all those Temple people would know there's something wrong….That's where your friend found me and took me one step further. He pulled me up on my feet and made me look at the world around me. He showed me that at least one person understood. And that was the start of something.

(Esther sits down on the other side of Mary.)

ESTHER: My experience was similar. When my dear husband died, oh, so many years ago, he left very little money in the bank. I did my best to manage on a fixed income, but one day, it just ran out. And then I realized that all the money

I had in the world, the little bit of cash I had to keep me alive, was just a pittance compared to the expendable profits of the wealthy. So I decided to go down to the Temple and put in my two cents, which is practically what it was. Granted, an old woman giving away the last little bit of money she has to live on is a pretty ineffectual protest, and it would have gone totally unnoticed, if your friend hadn't been there to point it out. He gave my actions a weight and a dignity they haven't had for many years, and I remember him for that.

MICAH: So you see, it did matter. It did make a difference, at least to us.

MARY: But it's over now. He's dead. Broken, buried, and stolen away. And it's all fading so fast. I can't even remember what he looked like anymore, and it's only been a couple of days. I don't remember anything he said, anything he did. In a little while I'll forget that I even knew him at all. And then it'll be over, like it never happened.

MICAH: Oh come on, you don't remember Jesus? That can't be true. You've got to remember when he started—all the preaching and the storytelling. Love and compassion and a new world at hand. A new world of justice. Remember that?

MARY: No. I don't remember.

ESTHER: And how the people heard the stories, but didn't understand, couldn't see what he was trying to show them.

MICAH: But that didn't stop Jesus. No siree. He started acting the stories out. He started healing the sick, and casting out demons, and hanging with the "undesirables," and all sorts of miraculous stuff. Remember?

MARY: No.

ESTHER:	And people were intrigued, but still they didn't understand. Didn't see what it meant to them.
MICAH:	But that didn't stop Jesus. No siree. He went straight to the city. Straight to the centre of power. He walked right into the Temple and took a stand. You must remember that. It was only a week ago. Remember?
MARY:	I told you, I don't remember!
MICAH:	*(Gesturing vaguely)* You remember. There was this guy? He was…you know, and kind of….He had this, what do you call it? One of those….Oh, come on, you remember.

> *(Mary looks at him blankly.)*
>
> *(For treatment 3—Money Changer enters and crowd enters milling about with improvisational character lines. Omit Micah's next 2 lines and actions. Crowd settles in sitting stage picture to watch and listen.)*

| MICAH: | Esther, give me that cap. |

> *(Esther pulls a visor out of her shopping bag and hands it to Micah.)*

| MICAH: | Now come on, you can't tell me you don't remember this guy. |

> *(Micah steps off to the side, puts on the visor, and plays the part of Money Changer.)*
>
> *(For treatment 3—from now on the Money Changer will take the Micah part with Micah standing aside watching.)*

| MICAH: | Pigeons for sale! Get them before they moult. Pigeons for sale! If you can't afford a decent sacrifice, pigeons are the next best thing. Can't do a purification rite without a pigeon. Perfect for the ladies. Get your pigeons here! |
| ESTHER: | Do you remember him? |

MARY: I…don't know.

> *(As Micah speaks he sets up or goes to an old TV table. He pulls a handful of coins out of his pocket and lays them out on the TV table.)*

MICAH: Who needs change? Good clean Jewish money for dirty Greek and Roman coins. Remember the rule: If it's got a face, it must be replaced! Can't have idolatrous coinage going into the Temple offering. Don't want to offend God with unclean money. And I think you'll find my exchange rates are on par with my competitors. Change here! Who needs change?

ESTHER: Do you remember, Mary? Do you remember what your friend said?

MARY: I…maybe?

> *(Esther takes the cloth out of Mary's hands. She unrolls it and drapes it over Mary's shoulders like a prayer shawl or a stole. She pulls Mary up and sets her before Micah/Money Changer.)*

> *(For treatment 3—Jesus enters—omit Esther/Mary cloth action—from here on the Mary part will be played by Jesus with Mary watching. * Means omit for treatment 3.)*

MICAH: *(Continuing his spiel)* Going on a trip? Need foreign currency? I'm your man. Good money for bad, bad money for good, whatever you need at competitive rates.

MARY: *(Hesitantly)* I…I want change. * *(Turning to Esther)** That's what he said.

ESTHER: * Indeed.

MARY: * I remember now. *(To Micah/Money Changer)* I want change.

MICAH:	Very good, sir. And what denominations will we be trading in today?
MARY:	What do you charge people for this little service?
MICAH:	My rates are competitive, sir.
MARY:	But you make a profit.
MICAH:	A man has to make a living.
MARY:	I see. And your clientele…a lot of poor people?
MICAH:	Not exclusively.
MARY:	But predominantly. And the pigeons?
MICAH:	Yes, the pigeons are mostly for the poor. And women and lepers. You're not interested in a pigeon, are you?
MARY:	How does it feel to be getting rich off the poor?

(Micah, as Money Changer, looks at Mary warily.)

MICAH:	I don't get rich, sir, I get by. And those who can't get by, sir, I pity. But if it's God's will that some should go poor, who am I to judge?
MARY:	Who's will is it that some should go poor?
MICAH:	God's, sir, of course.
MARY:	You lie! Now tell me, why are these people poor?
MICAH:	*(Getting angry)* It's not my job to ask why these people are poor. It's my job to provide a service. Now, do you want change or not?
MARY:	Yes! Yes, I do want change! I want this Temple to be a place of refuge for all people, like it's supposed to be. I want it to stop placing the needs of the institution above

the needs of the poor. I want people like you to stop exploiting the most vulnerable just to make a profit.

MICAH: Oh, get off your high horse…

MARY: It was a donkey. *(Keep this as Mary's line in treatment 3.)*

MICAH: I don't care what it was. I'm not a greedy profiteer, selling cheap merchandise out of a dark alleyway. I am a legitimate part of the Temple economy. I have official sanction and support. Without people like me, this Temple wouldn't run, and then where would your precious poor be? So don't treat me like a criminal, friend. I'm as much a part of this institution as any high priest.

(Mary pauses, slightly taken aback. She looks at Esther, and then back to Micah.)

MARY: So you all work together to gang up on the vulnerable. You help the rulers of the Temple oppress the poor, and they help you exploit them for a profit.

MICAH: Look, crazy man, I don't know what your problem is. I'm just a guy. A normal guy with a wife and kids. And I'm just trying to do my job.

(Slight pause.)

MARY: *(Apologetically)* You're right. I'm sorry.

(Mary starts to walk away.)

ESTHER: *Is that how it happened, Mary?

(Mary stops. Slight pause. She turns back to Money Changer.)

MARY: *(Calmly)* No. Not today you're not.

(She takes a corner of the TV table and flips it, sending the coins flying. In treatment 3 Crowd of Poor cheers.)

ESTHER: Hey!! Who do you think you are?

MARY: I'm Jesus.

(Esther has put on a large, impressive-looking hat, and now portrays the High Priest. In treatment 3 High Priest enters.)

ESTHER: What kind of a Jew are you? Disrupting the Temple and causing a disturbance. Don't you know there are people trying to pray. Have you no respect for religion? No respect for God?

MICAH: He's a Galilean, high priest, and you know what that means. You might as well call him an anarchist! All Galileans are alike.

(In treatment 3 the crowd reacts from now on, but without taking stage.)

ESTHER: Is that why you have come here, Jesus? To destroy the establishment, to undermine the government? You know that the Temple is the centre of the city's economy, and therefore, the country's. You know that this is where all the political, cultural, religious, and economic decisions are made. Is that why you're here? To destroy us?

MICAH: Round up your gang of cutthroat revolutionaries and get out of here! No wonder he kept talking about the poor. They're all criminals underneath.

MARY: Tell me, high priest, why must people who are poor come to this divided Temple? Why is there a place for the clean and a place for the unclean? A separate place for men of the right class, shape, and skin colour, and another place for women, for slaves, for cripples and lepers, and for the poor?

ESTHER: Every institution has an organizational structure. And, despite what you are trying to imply, the Temple is for everyone.

MARY: But why must they come here?

ESTHER: Why are you asking naive questions? They come because this is where God is. Where else should they go to pay their debts and seek forgiveness?

MARY: Forgiveness for what?

ESTHER: You know full well for what. For their sins.

MARY: You mean the sin of being poor.

ESTHER: If there wasn't something wrong with them, they wouldn't be poor, would they.

MARY: That is why I'm here! To stand against that obscenity! You define some as unclean, as second class citizens. Then you demand that they make amends for their second class status. And you both benefit from that arrangement!

> *(Micah takes a length of string and uses it to measure Mary for a cross, measuring first her height, then her arm span.)*

MICAH: *(Sarcastic and threatening)* Don't mind me, just taking a few measurements. This should be ready for you by Friday.

ESTHER: *(Momentarily unnerved)* You're just trying to intimidate me.

ESTHER: You'd be wise to heed his warning, Jesus.

MARY: No, you'd be wise to heed my warning! Those with the least suffer from this system, while those with the most prosper. The survival of the Temple is based on driving a wedge between the rich and the poor, and the poor end up getting poorer and poorer.

ESTHER: Are you an economist?…No, I didn't think so. Maybe you should stick to things you know something about. Go back to your preaching about love and morality. People like that. And stop being so rude and disruptive.

MARY: If I were polite and kept in my place, would anything change? Would the Temple become what it is supposed to be? According to the Torah we are to protect the poor, the vulnerable, and the outsiders. The Law calls us to…

ESTHER: Don't presume to tell me about the Law! I am high priest of the Temple. You don't tell me the Law, I tell you the Law. Now, you will leave, and you will stop making a nuisance of yourself, or I will be forced to summon a Roman soldier!

MARY: Check the holy of holies, high priest! God has leaked out. God has leaked out of the Temple and into the streets! God is flowing to lower ground. God is dwelling with the poor, with those who have been labelled unclean, with those who have been blamed for their situation.

ESTHER: I am warning you, Jesus.

MARY: God has left this place. But God will return. God will return when the Temple is once again a place of refuge and justice and compassion for the poor! And that will be a new beginning!

ESTHER: You know, you're only one man. You can't shut down the business of the Temple forever.

MARY: No, but I can shut it down for one day. And one day is enough to start.

(In treatment 3 Jesus exits and crowd follows.)

54

ESTHER: Indeed?

MARY: Indeed! *(In treatment 3 keep this as Mary's line.)*

            (Micah and Esther take off their hats and break out of character. Or in treatment 3, Money Changer and High Priest exit and Esther drapes the cloth Mary is holding around Mary's shoulders like a stole.)

MICAH: You see? You do remember.

MARY: That's what he said! That's what he did. I remember now.

MICAH: Of course. How could you forget?

MARY: I remember there was danger. Threats of punishment. Friendly advice to play it safe and keep a low profile.

MICAH: But that didn't stop Jesus. No siree. Jesus didn't back down, or run away.

MARY: Because God has anointed me to bring good news to the poor…

MICAH: Instead of blaming us for our poverty.

MARY: God has sent me to proclaim release to the captives…

MICAH: By treating us, not as second class citizens, but as people with dignity.

MARY: And recovery of sight to the blind…

MICAH: So that no one can say, "It's not my problem."

MARY: And to proclaim the year of God's favour.

MICAH: When there will be no rich, and there will be no poor, and the only law will be the Law of justice and compassion for all God's people.

ESTHER: Indeed. Which is exactly why they arrested him, and executed him as a criminal to the state, and buried his body in a cold stone tomb.

(Pause. Mary looks at Micah and Esther.)

MARY: *(Realizing)* But that didn't stop Jesus.

MICAH: *(Smiling)* No siree.

MARY: Because love is stronger than death. And justice is stronger than oppression.

ESTHER: And hope is stronger than despair.

MICAH: The tables turned, and the stone gets rolled away.

(Mary looks at herself, still wearing the linen cloth draped over her shoulders. She looks up at Esther.)

MARY: And Christ is risen.

ESTHER: *(Smiling)* Indeed.

MICAH: Indeed.

Summer

Summer like a breath
The universe in repose
Deep peace; deep longings

At Jacob's Well

A monologue by Esther Harris

Scripture and/or homily or meeting presentation based on John 4:5–30
Performance time: 10 minutes

CHARACTERS:
Woman at the well

TREATMENT AND SETTING:
This would be most effective learned and performed as a monologue with
the woman seated on a stool or standing. Or it could be done as a reading.
It deserves to be well done by someone with a feeling for poetry.

— • —

A funny thing happened
at Jacob's Well
one time
where I went
as was my wont
to draw water

Now that's a funny phrase
for which I plead your pardon
and any foot that I step on
whenever I use jargon

South of the border
except Mexico way
to draw water, they say
is everyday slang
cool as meringue
bespeaking that you cut some ice
which would be nice
for me to feel
that I counted

that I carried some weight
other than the jar
I fill each day
and carry away
from Jacob's Well

Yes, I go to Jacob's Well each day
and who
you well might ask
are you?

Let's leave me nameless for the nonce
an imprecise response no doubt
made with no wish, believe you me
to leaving you
out
in left field

Let me instead locate the Well
and tell you that it's found in Joseph's Field
an offspring piece of land
bequeathed to Joe by Jacob
an Artful kind of Dodger in his day
if ever there was one
perhaps learning from his mum
Rebekah
an old slyboots
much like her son

And my label?

Let's just say
my moniker, my handle,
my designation, appellation, or denomination
is simply
Samaritan

And one day
a weary man sat down beside the well
and said
Give me a drink

He said it to me
a woman of Samaria
who goes each day
to draw water
from Jacob's Well

Drawing a deep breath
I stared at the stranger
across Jacob's Well

That he spoke to me
left me stricken dumb

we each of us being
as foreign to the other
as the other could be

Normally, timidity is not within my ken
knowing what I know
of life and men

But

All sorts of thoughts flew through my head
and I saw scandal on the wing
with me coming in
for a crash landing
up against the rock-hard conventions
of two solitudes
his social traditions
and mine

Should I answer this man?
this foreigner who flouted conformity
who must know as surely as I
that no Jew has business
dealing with someone like me
a Samaritan
and a woman

besides—another jarring note
he'd also need to drink from
a Samaritan vessel
not a respectable receptacle
even when filled with water
drawn from Jacob's Well

So, curiously, riskily, at Jacob's Well
I boldly inquired
and asked him to tell:

"How is it that you, a Jew,
ask a drink of me,
a woman of Samaria?"

For the life of me
I never knew
such temerity
would go down
to posterity
as a quotable quote—I'll have you note
in the RSV
of the NOAB*

*1973—CE

Of course, at the time
I was stopped cold
in my tracks

as the rest of our talk
went right off the rails
and out of the window
went ties and restraints
boundaries of gender
and borders of race

for this was a man
whose words dazzled me
so
telling me things
he couldn't possibly know

that I'd had five spouses
was one thing he said
and never a judgement
on the reasons for this

I was convinced
the man was a seer
—truly a prophet—
who opened my eyes astonishingly so

I now could see
beyond the water in Jacob's Well

And whether you were chosen
or whether you were not
it mattered
neither a whit nor a jot that day
at Jacob's Well

Where a stranger offered me the water of life
before ever himself drank
a drop of the water
drawn out from Jacob's Well

Where the prophet I saw
encouraged me more in the questions I raised

theological questions
is the current thinking

but I simply wanted to ensure
I stood in a properly pure place
to worship
God
so enmeshed was I
in attitudes
of longitudes and latitudes

His answer
spiriting me away
to new heights of hope
dared me to raise
the most elevated topic
of them all
with this most perfect person

Was I witness
to Christ?
the Messiah?

I hardly heard his answer: "I who speak to you am he"
before other men hurried over, surrounded him, offered him food,
silently ignoring me

Excluded from their circle
I took my jar and left Jacob's Well
returning to the city with my testimony

Jonah

Peggy Freeman

Scripture drama based on the Book of Jonah
Performance time: 20 to 25 minutes

CHARACTERS:

Narrator
God—at an off-stage microphone or in view as a second narrator
Jonah
Sun (optional, but fun)
Sailors/Ninevites—(2) who manipulate wave fabric
Whale—3 actors

TREATMENT AND SETTING:

This play can be done with two narrators and all action in mime. However, breaking the narration with character lines, as indicated in the script, adds variety and challenge for the actors.

You could construct a whale—a very large cloth "whale bag" to be popped down over Jonah for him to struggle in. If you choose the three person human whale, I suggest dressing them in grey. You could accent their costumes as creatively as you like to expand on their whale appearance. Obviously, it will take a bit of rehearsal time to co-ordinate the combined whale and Jonah movements.

The sun could be dressed in bright yellow and might have a cut out of rays from foam rubber or card board with his or her face "shining" through the centre.

The sailors/ninevites remain in the centre aisle, throughout the play, at either end of a long piece of blue cloth ready to pick it up and bring it to life at the appropriate times (see workshop section). They should sit when not acting so as not to block the view.

This script is in rhyme, so work with your readers to put life and expression in the narration and avoid falling into a monotonous speaking pattern.

Your music director/facilitator might like to suggest appropriate songs for the congregation to sing at significant points in the drama, for fun and involvement.

— ◆ —

NARRATOR: The story of Jonah is about an ordinary man, who was called on, by God to do a job. Jonah didn't want to do the job at all, and he was very creative in finding ways to get out of it. Jonah was a man full of prejudice. He wanted God to love those that Jonah loved, and to hate those that Jonah hated. He could not imagine a God that loved everyone. Here's how Jonah handled his problem with God…and how God handled God's problem with Jonah.

NARRATOR: O Jonah was a man who had no special style at all,
(enter Jonah) He wasn't brave or bold…
he wasn't big and tall,
He had no special talent, he was just one of the mob.
But he's the one that God picked out to do a special job.

GOD: Hey Jonah, I'm asking you today
To take a message for me to a people far away
I know that you can do it, so I'm calling now you see.

NARRATOR: But Jonah said (what we all say),

JONAH: Oh Lordy, why pick me?

GOD: The Ninevites need saving from their wicked evil ways
Go, take the message Jonah and tell them that their days
and nights and all their future time is laying on the line.

JONAH: I'm busy God, maybe some other time.
I'm really not a preacher God,
you must know lots of men
who'd do a better job for you,
why don't you call on them.

GOD: Go and tell them to clean up their act.
They haven't got a lot of time and that's a fact.

NARRATOR: Well Jonah kept on saying no, he put up quite a fight.
(Jonah vigorously shakes head no.) The problem was he really didn't LIKE the Ninevites!

He thought it didn't matter if they got eliminated.
The fact that God asked him to go,
made him so irritated. *(Jonah stomps foot)*

God just kept on asking,
Jonah knew He wouldn't quit,
So finally Jonah thought that he would LIE a little bit.
Suppose…he just TOLD God he'd go,
then went the other way.
Boy, this sure sounds familiar! We do this everyday!

So Jonah bought a ticket on a sailboat shipping out.
He'd get away from God's request
of this he had no doubt.
A nice sea voyage would be grand—he'd rest
and read and fish.
The boat that Jonah boarded was going to Tarshish.

> *(Jonah leaves the front of the church and buys a ticket and runs down the centre aisle to where the waves are waiting to be activated. Jonah mimes pulling up sail and casting off.)*

NARRATOR: Jonah's plan was rather weak he thought he'd take a hike
And God would never find him
and THIS God wouldn't like
So he'd find ANOTHER preacher
to save those wretched sinners
Then the Ninevites and Jonah and God—
they'd all be winners.

> *(Waves begin to move gently. Sun enters and takes "warm, shining" position.)*

NARRATOR: The sun was shining warmly as they started on that trip
Old Jonah he felt mighty proud,
he'd given God the slip.
But then a storm came blowing
and the waves got very high.

(Sun exits.)

(Jonah interacts with the waves, ducking under to be on one side then another as his invisible boat bobs in the water.)

NARRATOR: The sailors feared that all on board
were simply going to die.
Lightening and thunder and wind and seas and rain
Jonah thought for sure he'd never see his home again.
A sailor said,

SAILOR 1:   There's someone here has caused this pretty mess.

SAILOR 2:   I think that someone better just come forward
and confess!

(The organ can make "storm" noises here.)

NARRATOR: So Jonah said,

JONAH: I'm much afraid this storm is due to me.
If you are wise you'll throw me and baggage in the sea.
For I have made God angry but this is not your fight.
No reason you should die because I hate the Ninevites.

(Jonah jumps forward and waves stop waving and drop to the floor immediately.)

NARRATOR: Jonah left the ship right then. He didn't stop to think.
It wouldn't do him any good to throw him in the drink.
As soon as Jonah left the ship the sun began to shine.
(Sun enters "shining.") The wind went down,
the waves did too and everything was fine.

But Jonah's troubles didn't stop
when he got off the boat.
For Jonah couldn't swim a stroke he couldn't even float!
He floundered and he choked and gasped
he felt that life was o'er *(Jonah flounders)*

When suddenly in front of him appeared a great red door.

(Whale appears—3 actors, arms linked with outside free arms stretched out to pull Jonah in. Whale goes down so that Jonah can be seen lounging comfortably in the centre.)

NARRATOR:　　He found himself inside that door 'twas nice
as he could wish.
He made himself quite comfortable—
there wasn't any choice.
And then he heard it very loud…somehow
he knew that voice.

GOD:　　"NOW WILL YOU GO TO NINEVEH?" *(Loudly!— Jonah reacts)*

NARRATOR:　　For three long nights and three long days
he had a fishy ride,
That whale knew that Jonah was sitting deep inside
Giving him a tummy-ache and clogging up his spout
He hoped he soon would have a chance to spit
the fellow out.

(Whale with Jonah in middle travels down centre aisle between moving waves. Whale tosses Jonah out and exits—waves stop.)

NARRATOR:　　As soon as it was possible he spat him on the beach
And Jonah got his courage up and he began to preach.

(Jonah moves to front and addresses audience.)

JONAH:　　Your time is running out…you've got to get it right
If you guys don't clean up your act
there'll be no Ninevites
Repent, change today your wicked, evil ways
Or God will knock your city down,
you've got just 40 days.

NARRATOR: Jonah thought the people would resist his warning cry
He thought the folks of Nineveh
were really going to die.
The Ninevites all listened—they put ashes on their heads
They dressed themselves in sackcloth
and to the Lord they said,

NINEVITES: Oh we are very sorry, please forgive the lives we've led
We are going to do better. Don't destroy us, please,
they said.

NARRATOR: Then God looked with compassion
on the people in the city
He saw that they were sorry and he was moved to pity.

GOD: I won't destroy you, for you have done what's right
You listened to my messenger, you are good Ninevites.

(Jonah reacts by taking a sulking/pouting stance that he holds to the end.)

NARRATOR: Now Jonah was an angry man,
he couldn't change his feelings
He thought God would destroy them
for all their evil dealings
But when they all repented and changed their evil ways
Poor Jonah sulked and pouted for days and days
and days.

So let's not be like Jonah and run away and hide
And keep our little petty hates all locked away inside
For God is God of all the world of every time and place
People of all lands on earth are offered heavenly grace.

(Sun enters and "shines" for two beats and then all exit.)

Death and Birth

A STORY OF HOPE AND PENTECOST

Carolyn Pogue

Homily or sermon at the Easter season or anytime
Performance time:
Treatment 1—12 minutes; Treatment 2—18 minutes

CHARACTERS:
TREATMENT 1
Philip
Chloe

TREATMENT 2
Philip
Chloe
Crowd—to include at least five women (one of whom is **Jesus' mother**) and **several men** (one of whom is **Jesus**)

TREATMENT:

1. As storytelling or a dialogue between Philip and Chloe, perform as written—learned and staged or readers sitting theatre style on stools using music stands for the scripts.

2. As storytelling dialogue interspersed with interaction with other characters, as though happening now, for more dramatic tension and a larger cast.

SETTING:
A table in a central spot with pieces of pottery on it—perhaps a Money Changer's table elsewhere.

COSTUMES:
The characters may be fully dressed in biblical period costume or wear a suggestion of costume, for example, an appropriate headress, shawl, or scarf for each character. Or Chloe and Philip could dress in one colour, the crowd in another colour, and Jesus in a third colour. Or Jesus could dress in a solid colour and all other characters wear a scarf or other accessory of that colour. Or Philip and Chloe and Jesus could wear modern dress and the other characters could wear biblical dress.

—◆—

(Philip and Chloe, in the front of the nave, speak primarily to the audience throughout the play.)

PHILIP:	We were there. We saw it happen.
CHLOE:	We have to tell the story before it is lost
PHILIP:	or before we die
CHLOE:	or before we forget. *(aside)* We'd better tell them who we are.
PHILIP:	Oh. Of course. This is Chloe.
CHLOE:	And this is Philip.
PHILIP:	There. We did that. Where were we?
CHLOE:	We were saying we need to tell the story before it is lost.
PHILIP:	Ah, yes. You don't know us, but we were there, and we know what really happened, you see. We met them here, in Jerusalem.
CHLOE:	I was helping at the market, selling Philip's pottery. He's a wonderful potter, you know.
PHILIP:	You really think so?
CHLOE:	You're fishing my dear. It was an ordinary day, a Wednesday, I think.
PHILIP:	Business was a little slow. I remember thinking, "Has everyone suddenly got enough bowls? Enough jugs for water and wine? Isn't anyone breaking dishes any more?"
CHLOE:	So we were just talking with the people at the next stall, the ones who sell sandals. Like I said, it was an ordinary day.

PHILIP: Sunny, warm. No breeze.

CHLOE: A few flies buzzing around. It was morning. Then, off to the left, we heard someone preaching.

PHILIP: I didn't pay attention at first. This is Jerusalem, after all. Preachers are a shekel a dozen. Everybody and his brother is a prophet around here.

Treatment 2

CHLOE: *(Moves, on line, to one side where "stall" with pottery is preset.)* But so many people went to hear this guy that the market was quiet enough that his voice carried. We didn't plan to listen, but...

PHILIP: *(joining Chloe)* it was impossible not to hear.

> *(Crowd enters with crowd noise, improvised lines, and then they hush one another as all gaze intently up at Jesus who has entered the pulpit and they strike a stage picture. There should be a designated Esther and Eliham in the crowd.)*

CHLOE: Some of what he said made sense.

PHILIP: And some of what he said made me wonder why the Romans didn't knock his head off.

CHLOE: *(whispering)* There have been enough crucifixions around here. It's their favourite way to kill us. Just thinking about it brings back the smell to my nostrils. It makes me sick.

PHILIP: When we went home that night, I wondered if we'd see him on a cross soon. I mean, he didn't mince any words.

CHLOE: The crowds were back the next day.

PHILIP: *(Shows pottery to some disinterested members of the*

Crowd.) Not to buy my pottery, though. There was a knot of people around him.

CHLOE: Two of them, we discovered, were people we knew. Esther's girl, Anne. The wild one. The prostitute.

PHILIP: The other was Eliham, one of the worst cheats I've ever known. Last year he went straight and I didn't know why. Turns out that the two of them are this preacher man's friends. Both of them straight as arrows now.

CHLOE: They came by the stall and talked to us for a while.

(Esther and Eliham stand facing Chloe and Philip in front of their stall.)

PHILIP: Made us sit up and think, you know. Made us wonder. *(pause)* When he came to Jerusalem for a few days or a few weeks, he'd preach in the temple or the market. He even went outside the gates where the outcasts and lepers are. Who ever heard of such a thing? *(Jesus exits with all but Chloe and Philip following.)*

CHLOE: To make a long story short, we started to listen to him, too. His name is Jesus. Heard his interpretation of Torah. Heard what he thought about the mess we're in now with the...you know? *(She glances over her shoulder)*...the powers. *(pause)* Funny thing is, he's a listener too. He shocked me when he looked me square in the face and talked to me like I was...a man *(gesturing to Philip)*, like him. Like I was somebody. He asked me what I thought!

PHILIP: We saw him fairly often.

CHLOE: Well, once we got used to his ideas and the people around him and all. Then Philip invited him to stay with us when he came to town.

PHILIP: No. It was you, Chloe. You invited him to stay with us.

CHLOE: *(Smiles and glances at him.)* Really.

PHILIP: So he and his friends stayed with us whenever they came to the city. We have extra room, you see. Sometimes we had a great big party. Other times it was just a few us talking. Sometimes they were so exhausted they just slept. Jesus sure wore out a lot of sandals. My neighbour got the idea to make him some for free. He'd always have an extra pair at our house for him.

CHLOE: I planted more vegetables in the garden, too. Those people could eat! But the cooking wasn't a burden. In fact it was fun. Everybody helped out with the cooking and cleaning up. It was like a family reunion whenever they came.

Treatment 2 *(**Crowd re-enters with Mary and Jesus leading all, silently relating to one another, slowly moving across the chancel and exiting the other side during Philip's and Chloe's lines.**)*

PHILIP: It wasn't long before we met Mary, his mother.

CHLOE: Now, there's a woman you should know. She's gutsy and wise, and she can wear out a pair of sandals with the best of them.

PHILIP: Like us, her children are all grown up. But this one, her first born, is the one who keeps her from sitting at home in a rocking chair, which is where she really should be at her age. But no, here she is, marching around with her number one son and his band of revolutionaries. Amazing. *(**Crowd exits.**)*

CHLOE: Well. We saw them off and on over the period of a year. Sometimes we got reports that they were in trouble for breaking the rules. Other times we heard that Jesus was attracting great crowds because of his healing. Sometimes, though, we heard nothing. That was the worst.

PHILIP:	He was outstripping a lot of the other wandering preach-ers. His crowds were bigger. People who knew about him either loved or hated him.
CHLOE:	It was just before Passover that he came the last time. I wasn't there, but I heard that he caused a terrible scene in the temple. I was afraid for him. He couldn't afford to make a scene.
Treatment 2	***(You could have a preset Money Changer's table and pause in this script to enact the over-turning of the table with Jesus and a member of the Crowd as Money Changer using the appropriate scripture lines.)***
PHILIP:	We invited him for the Passover meal, but he said he wanted to spend it with just the twelve. We understood.
CHLOE:	We helped by preparing the food for them and then leaving them alone.
PHILIP:	My last glimpse of him he was washing John's feet. Imagine. We went over to Priscilla and Andrew's next door. But we all felt uneasy. It was hard to concentrate. We didn't sleep well that night, either. We were waiting.
CHLOE:	Waiting for what? We didn't know, exactly. Just waiting.
PHILIP:	You know how it feels when you see black clouds scuttling across the desert or the fields? You know that the storm is coming, and there is nothing to stop the wind from bringing it. Waiting is hard. Do you know what I mean? *(reflective gaze)*
Treatment 1	
CHLOE:	It was Salome who banged on our door in the morning. She said he'd been arrested.
PHILIP:	The sun was shining, but I was so cold. I was shivering.

CHLOE: We went to find Peter but we couldn't. We found Mary Magdalene. She said they'd taken Jesus to Caiphus' house for questioning and then on to Pilate. It looked bad. Mary saw him. He'd been beaten, she said.

PHILIP: We knew we couldn't do anything for Jesus,

CHLOE: so we went to find his mother. She was in the court of the women at the temple, praying. We just sat with her.

PHILIP: Until Mary, James' mother came to find us. "It is the end,"—is what she said. "There is no hope." We went to find the others. At a time like this, you can't be alone.

Treatment 2 *(Mary enters and kneels in prayer to the side. Sound of door banging. Salome enters.)*

SALOME: *(to Chloe and Philip)* He's been arrested!

PHILIP: Arrested? The sun is shining brightly, but suddenly it feels so cold.

CHLOE: Where's Peter has anyone seen him or Mary Magdalene?

(Mary M. enters running—the others greet her.)

MARY M: They've taken Jesus to Caiphus' house for questioning and then on to Pilate! It looks bad. I saw him, he's been beaten.

PHILIP: We can't...do anything for Jesus

CHLOE: Let's find his mother and wait with her. She's usually in the court of the women at the temple praying, at this time.

(Chloe, Salome and Mary M. join Mary and sit with her. Mary, James' mother enters and speaks to the women and to Philip, who is nearby.)

MARY, JAMES' MOTHER: It is the end. There is no hope.

PHILIP: We must find the others. At a time like this no one should be alone. *(Philip and all the others exit.)*

Treatment 1 and 2

CHLOE: *(re-enters down the centre aisle)* Do you know what's it's like to be in shock? You hear differently. The air is different, even. Things are more in focus, sharper. And yet there is an unreal quality to it all. I remember noticing strange things, little things. Like, I noticed the sparrows on the cobblestones just outside the temple. A dozen of them maybe. Hopping around, eating crumbs and grit from between the stones. Fluttering up, then landing again, like it was an ordinary day. But they seemed unreal in the too-bright sun.

PHILIP: *(if treatment 2, enter and join Chloe)* They'd beaten him alright. He was bleeding and his mouth was torn where they'd smashed his face. They'd given him a crown of thorns. His legs trembled as he tried to carry that cross. It was hot. *(pause)*

CHLOE: His mother pushed her way to the front of the crowd in the street. She wanted him to see her. I don't know what she said, but I know she spoke to him.

PHILIP: And then they nailed him to the cross and the world ended and hope disappeared. And he died. *(pause)*

CHLOE: I'm sure you've heard of Mary Magdalene's announcement? That she saw him alive?

PHILIP: And afterwards he appeared to the eleven. I tell you that for a month after, there were rumours and stories and miracles happening and people fainting and praying and I don't know what all.

CHLOE: We didn't know what to think.

PHILIP: Some of the friends went back home and said they were going to forget the whole thing. You couldn't blame them.

CHLOE: Others had nowhere to go. They'd given up everything. I'd see some of them hanging around in the market or going to the temple. They looked blank.

PHILIP: The worst were the ones who kept looking over their shoulders, waiting for something to happen to them.

CHLOE: It was awful.

PHILIP: Some stayed in Jerusalem. Others wandered out of town. *(pause)* Then one day,

CHLOE: the disciples came back. It was Peter who told us. "Jesus has been taken into heaven," he said.

PHILIP: Whatever that means.

CHLOE: One thing it meant to me is that the whole thing was really over. People were just going to have to get on with it. Get back to normal. I mean, what else can you do?

PHILIP: James asked if they could use our roof as a meeting place. Chloe said yes.

CHLOE: No, it was you who said yes, Philip. I remember.

PHILIP: Are you sure? I thought it was you. I was scared.

CHLOE: I was scared too. Would I have said yes? Put us in danger like that?

PHILIP: Well. It was a confusing time.

CHLOE: Terrifying.

PHILIP: You jumped when anyone knocked at the door.

CHLOE: Your stomach turned to mush if a stranger looked at you funny or the soldiers glanced your way. We were all skittish.

PHILIP: You'd find yourself whispering. Even in bed.

CHLOE: But when they asked to meet here, what could we say?

PHILIP: We had loved Jesus, but he was executed for stirring up trouble.

CHLOE: If the authorities realized that the meetings were still going on…

            (Philip draws a line across his throat to signify death.)

CHLOE: Yes. The men came alone the first night. The next night, who's at the door, but Mary, mother of James, Salome, Mary Magdalene, Joanna, some of the others, and his mother!

Treatment 2   *(Crowd/Followers enter silently and gather around Philip and Chloe in stage picture during this speech.)*

PHILIP: I was shocked. Everyone thought she'd just fade away. Die of grief. We hadn't really known her, you see.

CHLOE: She was there. Strong.

PHILIP: Usually, we joined the group.

CHLOE: Sometimes we argued

PHILIP: or sang

CHLOE: or prayed the Psalms.

PHILIP: We supported each other, you see.

            (Chloe and Philip and Crowd move into nave and Crowd sits in pews as Chloe and Philip speak.)

CHLOE:	We went with the group at Pentecost. After all the running and hiding over the past few weeks, we were flabbergasted that so many showed up. And you said, "The Jesus movement is still alive!"
PHILIP:	No, you said that.
CHLOE:	Are you sure? I thought it was you. *(She laughs.)*
	(The speed and energy builds from here to "and again" and "and again.")
Treatment 2	*(The Crowd, now in the pews improvise excited whispering to one another, slowly building in energy but remaining a whisper, under the following lines. Philip and Chloe might begin moving down the centre aisle for a more intimate relationship with the audience especially if remote microphones are available.)*
PHILIP:	So that's how it was. Lots of people, hundreds, and a buzz in the air, you know? Excitement! Everyone talking at once. We were waiting again.
CHLOE:	And again, we didn't know what we were waiting for. But this time, it was different.
PHILIP:	There wasn't even a place to sit down, there were so many of us. Even new people came!
CHLOE:	So, I don't know, one minute we were singing a hymn, a fast one, one with energy.
PHILIP:	And we were all holding hands.
CHLOE:	And there was this warm, wild wind, remember?
PHILIP:	and it was like the world was split wide open with love and hope
CHLOE:	We were on fire

81

PHILIP: and Peter made a speech, and we applauded until our hands were red and then the women formed circles and started to dance *(You might wish to play a rendition of the Magnificat very softly under the following speeches.)*

CHLOE: and the men formed circles around us and danced, too. And Philip was laughing and shouting, "Not even the Romans can kill this!"

PHILIP: I said that?

CHLOE: Yes, Philip, you did.

PHILIP: So we knew then, and we know now, that you cannot kill love with nails and crosses

CHLOE: not with hate

PHILIP: or power built on the backs of others.

CHLOE: Eventually

PHILIP: in the end

CHLOE: Mary's Magnificat will come true again

PHILIP: and again

CHLOE: and again.

> *(Whispering and music subsides. Chloe and Philip take deep breaths and then proceed at normal pace.)*

PHILIP: So, although we were there at the death,

CHLOE: we were also there at the birth

PHILIP: of whatever it was

CHLOE: that made us stay together.

PHILIP: We are not alone.

CHLOE: *(and all other characters from where they are seated)* Thanks be to God.

PHILIP: And that's our story.

First Things First

Peg Cox and Elizabeth Symon

Scripture and homily or meeting
Relevant scripture: Luke 10:38–42 and Luke 12:22–31
Performance time: 6 to 8 minutes

CHARACTERS:

Martha
Mary

TREATMENT AND SETTING:

Use the centre of the chancel around a table or the altar. Place a large welcome mat at the top of the chancel step (upside down from point of view of the congregation). Have the communion silver and a folded table cloth on the table or altar. I suggest miming the phone, but you could use a real one if you prefer. Martha should wear a large apron and Mary could carry a book and wear earphones and a Walkman.

If this play is being performed at a meeting, include a potluck supper and use the food table as the focus.

— • —

MARTHA:	*(Coming in from the garden with a basket.)* Was that the phone, Mary?
MARY:	*(Book in hand)* Yes, we've got a guest for supper. It's…
MARTHA:	At this short notice! I wonder if I've picked enough fruit and vegetables then? And I suppose I'm going to have to bake some more bread! Oh, dear! I do hope young Peter next door will remember to defrost the salmon he's been promising us. We can have it for the main course.
MARY:	Martha! You never even asked who's coming! *(Begins reading her book silently.)*
MARTHA:	I just can't relax when a guest's due. All the extra cleaning and cooking to be done. Hmm. Baked or scalloped potatoes? Mary, I do wish you'd listen for once!

MARY: He'll be here soon, he said, he's on his way to
_____(*local place*). He's been talking to a group of
young people at _____(*local group*).

MARTHA: Well, one thing's for sure. I'm going to need your help,
my girl. You've always got your nose stuck in one of
those books from church, or earphones on, listening to
tapes. I'm left to do everything myself, it seems.

MARY: Look at the doormat. There now, welcome reads the
right way round now. How's that? (*Turns mat around.*)

MARTHA: That's a fine welcome! Look at the dust on the mat! You
just get our visitor to take off his shoes at the door, like
anyone else. We don't want any more dirt tramped into
the house.

MARY: We'll ask him to say grace, won't we?

MARTHA: First things first, my girl. I don't suppose there's a clean
tablecloth?

MARY: This one? (*Lifts up cloth lying on the table.*)

MARTHA: No, that needs ironing…and I don't have time to do that
too. We'll have to use placemats. Oh, dear, the silver
needs polishing! I wonder if one bottle of wine will be
enough? It's all we've got. Oh, and the glasses need
washing! (*Refer to communion items.*)

MARY: Don't worry so much, Martha! Remember the wedding
at Cana, when they ran short of wine, and served some
that looked just like water, but it tasted out of this
world?

MARTHA: Well, never mind that story now. Look at the time!
(Glances at watch.) I'll never be ready! We've got this
special guest coming, who phoned over an hour ago, you

say, and now you're not even helping! You know I can't do everything myself!

MARY: There's the phone again! I'll answer it. *(Picks up phone and listens.)* Hello...Yes...*(To Martha)* Martha, the meeting at _____*(local place)* is over, and He'll be right here. I'm going to ask Him if I can become a disciple! *(Holds hand over phone.)*

MARTHA: He's not bringing all of his disciples with him, I hope!

MARY: No, don't worry! He's by himself. He said not to go to any great trouble on his behalf: just open a can of tuna, and spread it on some rolls. We could eat picnic style on a TV table, or outside on the porch, couldn't we? With some wine or juice, while we talk together? *(Quotes)* "Wine that gladdens the heart, and bread that sustains the heart." Didn't he say that nicely? He knows the Bible so well. I wish I did!

MARTHA: You mean *(slowly)* no fancy spread, just SAND-WICHES? I'm not to provide a feast, like the church women do for the men's fellowship?

MARY: That's right! *(Then, on phone.)* Yes, Martha's here. She's busy in the kitchen.

MARTHA: Let me have that phone, please! *(Talking into the phone.)* Yes, it's Martha! It's the same old story. My sister's left me to do all the work by myself. Could you please tell her to come right now and help me, now there're all these sandwiches to make....Oh, there's the kettle, boiling its head off. And I'm the only one to see to it! Bye! *(Hangs up phone.)*

MARY: I'll tell you what he said, Martha. It's in the Bible. *(Reads)* "Don't worry about food...life is more important than that. Think of the birds—they don't plant seeds or gather a harvest, and they don't have storage rooms or barns. God feeds them! Human beings are worth more than birds…Can any one of us live longer by worrying? You mustn't make yourself upset worrying what we'll eat and drink…Our creator knows we need these things. Instead, we need to be concerned about God's realm. God will provide for us."

MARTHA: Hmm, that sounds good! Okay, then, I'll just take off my apron, and come and sit down and take it easy…everything else can wait! *(Sits)*

> *(If it is to be a communion service, have someone bring forward the bread and wine at this time.)*
>
> *(If it is a potluck supper, have some people put their food items on the table throughout the following speech.)*

MARY: *(Going to door and looking out.)* Martha, here's Peter now with the salmon! It's been cooked, and his mother's made us some baking powder biscuits! I've asked them both to stay for supper with us! *(Puts items on the table, then looks out again.)* And look, there's our brother Lazzy just getting off his motorcycle with some shopping—he must have picked up on his way home from work! Lazzy must've stopped at _____ *(local store)*. He's brought us an apple pie and a bucket of ice cream!

MARY: And our special guest is just coming up the path—and see, He's brought us some flowers—just "lilies of the field," he says, but aren't they beautiful! And I'll set the table! We'll be one big family!

MARTHA: *(Reflectively)* Now why did I get so worked up, I wonder? Guess I've been like a camera on the wrong setting—no wonder everything seemed out of focus for me!

MARY: You can say that again!

MARTHA: And now, first things first, if our special guest will lead
               us in the blessing,

               (If this play is being performed in a worship service.)

BOTH: "The peace of God, which passes all understanding, keep
               our hearts and minds through Jesus Christ, Amen" *(or
               another version of The Peace).*

MARY: The peace, Martha!

MARTHA: The peace, Mary.

               *(Mary and Martha hug each other, then ask the
               congregation to pass the peace themselves.)*

— ◆ —

If this play is being done at a potluck supper—both lead the gathering
in a grace that is known to all. And then enjoy the food!

The Call of Moses

Gary Paterson and Keri K. Wehlander

Scripture drama based on Exodus 3:1–4:17
Performance time: 4 minutes

CHARACTERS:
God
Moses

TREATMENT:
This is a playful dialogue between God and Moses. They address one another, but reveal their inner thoughts to the congregation. Take time to have fun with these characters, developing Moses' nervousness and God's exasperation. The only prop needed is God's long staff. You could use costumes or not. In my opinion costumes are not necessary for this drama.

It should be noted that most of Moses' lines to God are taken directly from the Biblical passage.

SETTING:
Keep it simple. The two characters in a central area is all that is needed; a balcony would be a good mountain top if the characters can be seen.

— • —

GOD: *(Holding a long staff, signals Moses to come closer.)*
                Moses, take off your shoes!

                (Moses takes off shoes—demonstrating nervousness by looking for a place to put them, finally finding somewhere or deciding to keep hold of them.)

GOD: Moses, I have heard the cry of the Israelites. I have seen how the Egyptians have oppressed them. They need to be set free from their bondage! Moses, I have chosen you to lead them out of slavery into a land of promise, a land flowing with milk and honey.

MOSES: *(Aside to congregation)* I should have known better than to check out that burning bush—nothing but trouble, big time. Go to Egypt?! Oh sure! Easy for God to say. I've got to get out of this!

(Turning to God) Who am I that I should go to Pharaoh, and bring the Israelites out of Egypt?

GOD: *(Aside to congregation)* I should have listened to my first instinct about this guy. He's got that kind of scruffy, unreliable look to him, you know?

(Turning to Moses) Moses, I will be with you—and you will lead the people of Israel to this place, to this very mountain. And when you have reached this mountain, you all will worship me here.

MOSES: *(Aside to congregation)* Fat chance! If I go to Egypt, that's the end of me—there's no getting out. Chariots and soldiers everywhere! (Pauses for a moment.) You know, I think God really is serious about all this—I'm getting worried.

(Turning to God) If I come to the Israelites and say to them, "the God of your ancestors has sent me to you," and they ask me, "what is your name?" What shall I say to them?

GOD: *(Bows to Moses)* I am who I am.

MOSES: *(Aside to congregation)* Right! Ask God a straightforward question and what do you get: "I Am Who I Am"! What kind of a name is that! Get real!

(Turning to God) And suppose they don't believe me or listen to me, but say, "God did not appear to you!"

GOD: *(Aside to congregation)* Excuses, excuses. Humans! They're all alike. Now zebras—they're different. Every time I ask one of my zebras to do something—zip!— they're off and running!

(Turning to Moses.) Moses, I will enable you to perform three signs. *(Holds staff out to Moses.)* You will be able to place this staff on the ground, and it will turn into a snake. Then, when you pick it up by the tail, it will turn back into a staff. You will also be able to place your hand inside your cloak, and it will come out covered with leprosy. Then, all you have to do is put it back inside your cloak and it will come out without any trace of the leprosy. And the third sign that I will enable you to perform is that you will be able to take water from the Nile, pour it on the dry ground, and it will turn into blood. *(God demonstrates in mime these signs as they are described.)*

MOSES: *(Aside to congregation)* Hey, this looks exciting! Snakes, leprosy, blood! It'll sure make everyone take a second look at me. Not bad!

> *(Moses goes one step towards God, as if to take the staff, pauses, and then turns quickly back to congregation.)*

Wait a minute! That was close! I almost said yes, and there's still the small problem of a million Egyptian chariots. Quick! I've got to think!

(Turning to God piteously.) O my Lord, I have never been eloquent, neither in the past nor even now that you have spoken to your servant; I am slow of speech and slow of tongue.

GOD: *(Aside to congregation)* Now that's an understatement if I ever heard one!

(Turning to Moses) Moses, Moses! Look at me! Who invented speech? Betcha if I invented it, betcha I could help you with it!

MOSES: *(Aside to congregation)* Well, yes, but, but...

(Turning to God with a desperate tone.) Oh my Lord! Please send someone else!

GOD: *(Aside to congregation)* Behold! This man Moses is increasing my wroth...greatly!

(Turning to Moses) Moses! Enough of this! Your brother Aaron speaks with ease and eloquence. You will go and tell him what I have told you, and then I will teach the two of you what to do as we go along. I have chosen you! *(Gives Moses the staff.)* That's all you need to know! Now, GO!

(God turns and leaves.)

MOSES: *(After a moment of deliberation.)*
Who am I to say "no"?

(Moses or choir sings "Who Am I" or other appropriate song or hymn and congregation joins in.)

The Welcome Mat

(FROM A ONCE OVERHEARD WISDOM STORY)

Louise Smith

Sermon or homily or meeting
Performance time: 4 to 6 minutes

CHARACTERS:

Narrator
Abraham
Stranger—an older man
Sarah
Off Stage Voice

TREATMENT AND SETTING:

It would be effective simply as a dialogue with set and props mimed if the actors have some abilities in mime technique. They could be dressed in casual modern dress—perhaps Abraham and Sarah in one colour and the Stranger in another.

Or a somewhat fuller staging could be done with a table, three chairs, a pitcher filled with water, and a loaf of bread. The stranger will need a pack containing cloth to rummage through and a large idol. The actors could be in biblical dress or just biblical accessories—desert headdress etc.

You might like to experiment with two people using a long, possibly green, cloth just up stage of the actors and table. (See workshop section of this book.) This cloth, in motion, could represent both the tent and the cool, refreshing hospitality of Abraham and Sarah's home.

Pick a hot summer day to do this play so that the audience will appreciate the need for the refreshment.

— ◆ —

NARRATOR: Long, long ago, in biblical times, it was very important to make others feel welcome. You must remember, this was in a time and place where it was very hot. There was not much soft, green grass or cool and shady branches hanging overhead. It was sandy, dusty, and hot. When folks would walk in the heat of the day, their throats would get scratchy from the sand and dust blowing in

93

their face. If a stranger were to happen by, you would offer them refuge in the coolness of your tent, and quench their thirst with a mug of cold, cold water. This was exactly what happened to Abraham one day, when a stranger wandered by.

(Cloth action begins—try allowing the cloth to rise gently to its full height and then fall softly down. Repeat this action with an established rhythm behind Abraham and Sarah at the table.)

(Stranger enters down stage.)

ABRAHAM: Good day sir. It's too hot to remain outdoors for long. Please, please, come into my home.

NARRATOR: With this, Abraham beckoned the stranger into his tent. He called out to his wife Sarah.

ABRAHAM: Sarah, we have a visitor. Fetch some cold water. And fetch some bread as well. Our visitor looks tired and hungry.

SARAH: Yes Abraham, I'll go at once.

NARRATOR: Within minutes Sarah returned and began to set a table. She poured cool, glistening water in the tall ceramic mugs. She broke the bread and let it rest in the centre of the table. With that, she looked at Abraham and gave him a quick nod.

ABRAHAM: Ah. The table is ready. First, my friend, we shall give thanks to the One who has so graciously provided us with this food and drink.

NARRATOR: The stranger nodded his approval and began to slowly and carefully open his pack. Abraham and Sarah watched with curiosity. Never had they seen anyone dig through their belongings before offering a blessing. Finally the stranger pulled an object wrapped in cloth from his bag and for the first time, he spoke.

STRANGER: I do not believe in your God. I have my own God to worship.

NARRATOR: With these words, the stranger pulled from under the cloth a large, wooden idol.

STRANGER: It is not my custom to thank your God for the bountiful food. I must thank my God.

NARRATOR: With this the stranger bent down to pay homage to his wooden idol. This infuriated Abraham. With great anger he lashed out at the stranger.

ABRAHAM: You are worshipping a piece of wood. It is blasphemous to worship anything created with the human hand. Now get out of my house. You are an idiot and you have angered me and my God. Get out!

(Cloth action stops!)

NARRATOR: With that the stranger grabbed up his idol and pack and quickly left the tent. Abraham was still seething when a voice echoed in his ears.

VOICE: *(Off stage at a microphone.)* Abraham, you have made a grave error. You should not have sent that man away.

ABRAHAM: But I had to. He made a mockery of you God. He worshipped a silly wooden idol. Everyone knows it is blasphemous to worship idols.

VOICE: Yes, I heard him. But Abraham, he is an old, old man and I have been following him for many years. He knows no better than to worship that silly wooden idol, but Abraham, he is still a child of mine. He knows no better, but you my friend, you do. Now go. Fetch the old man and make him welcome once again.

NARRATOR: With that Abraham ran after the old man. *(Pause in narration while Abraham runs after and brings back the Stranger.)* When he reached him, he apologized for his misconduct and once again made the offering of shade, food, and water in his home. *(Cloth action resumes and continues to the end.)* On that day, in that hot and blistering sun, Abraham learned a valuable lesson. It is not his place in the world to make judgements on another person's beliefs. And he did as God asked him. He brought back the stranger and once again made him feel welcome.

Autumn

Autumn like wisdom
colours our understandings
and ripens our faith

Naomi

A monologue by Betty Radford Turcott

A harvest reflection for worship or meeting
Performance time: Approximately 4 minutes

CHARACTERS:
Naomi
A Young Woman in the congregation

TREATMENT AND SETTING:
A woman in the autumn of her life is seated in a comfortable chair in the centre of the chancel. She is in modern dress. She is the Naomi of biblical times and the Naomi of today. It can be read, but will be more effective learned and performed.

You may wish to precede this drama with a reading from the Book of Ruth.

You may wish to involve a musician to fade some appropriate music in and out during this piece—perhaps something with a gentle constant beat.

— • —

(Naomi is creating, either weaving at a loom or knitting or some similar activity. She is reflecting on her life with thanksgiving.)

NAOMI: How beautiful the threads are! How rich and lovely the fabric that is coming to life. Strands of colour woven together into a beautiful pattern. It is so true to life. We work and we live, we suffer and we survive. Then in the autumn of our lives we hand the pattern on to those who follow us. We received from the old ones who have gone before and we hand on to the lives that are to follow. Autumn, to winter, to spring.

Whatever we create with our hands, needs to be shaped and formed and moulded. So it is with the pattern of our living. My life was shaped by many, many events. The

99

journey into a foreign land and the creation of a new life there with my husband and my sons. We were blessed with gracious wives for our sons. They added joy and laughter to our home and we were ready for new life, for fulfilment. But instead, of growth, it was a time of pruning, of cutting and reshaping. It was a time of falling away, like leaves in the autumn. Death took our husbands, Orpah's and Ruth's and mine, and we felt the pain of loss.

We lived in that pain for a long time. At last, I remembered the Temple song, and I lifted my eyes to the hills seeking strength. I had to learn to trust the rhythms of life again. The rhythms of life after life. It took time before I again could feel that pulsing movement within. And with it came the need to return to Bethlehem. Ruth and I went on that long journey. For me, it was a return to old patterns. For Ruth, a whole new pattern.

In the autumn of my days, I pass on to Ruth the fabric of faith and life in our village. It is a time of healing for me. The bitterness of the past gives way to trust in the future. The pain of the past becomes a promise of joy for tomorrow. As I held my grandson for the first time, I knew that joy.

Harvest time is once again upon the land and upon all of life. Thanks be to the one who brings the light of spring after the dark of autumn and winter days. The fabric of life is rich and beautiful. The pattern is as old as all our yesterdays, and as new as all our tomorrows.

(She rises and walks to a young woman in the congregation and lovingly passes on the unfinished creation to her.)

A Meeting at the Post Office

barb janes

Sermon or meeting
Performance time: 10 to 12 minutes

CHARACTERS:
Dorothy—in her sixties
Wendy—young mother
Helen—in her sixties

TREATMENT AND SETTING:
Two stools in the centre of the chancel.

— • —

DOROTHY:	*(Enters)* Why, hello, Wendy.
WENDY:	Oh, hi, Mrs. Simpson. *(Rises from stool)*
DOROTHY:	Oh, Wendy, you can call me Dorothy, you know. *(Sits on other stool)*
WENDY:	Sorry, Dorothy. No matter how old I get, I still call my mom's friends Mrs. whoever. *(Sits down again)*
DOROTHY:	I heard they're having trouble getting Sunday school teachers again. You must have a really big class this year.
WENDY:	Uh…no, I don't.
DOROTHY:	But last Sunday they said they only had three teachers, and there were, oh, there must have been forty children there.
WENDY:	I'm not teaching this year.

DOROTHY: Oh, Wendy, what a shame! I really enjoyed it when your class came upstairs last year and sang, "This Is my Father's World." They were so sweet. It brought back so many memories of when I was that age.

WENDY: (*Steeling herself*) Mrs. Simpson, that's one of the reasons I'm not teaching this year.

DOROTHY: Oh, now, I know it's a lot of work to get the children prepared for these things. When I was a teacher, it was my job to run the school Christmas pageant, and that was a job and a half, I can tell you. But everybody appreciated it. Just like everybody appreciated your class singing, "This Is My Father's World."

WENDY: The class didn't appreciate it. And neither did I.

DOROTHY: Wendy, whatever do you mean?

WENDY: The Superintendent got pressure from an 'influential' group for the kids to do something cute, those were their very words, 'something cute' upstairs. The children hated it. They were embarrassed.

DOROTHY: Why should they be embarrassed to sing one of the great songs of our faith?

WENDY: It's not their music. And it may not even be their faith.

DOROTHY: (*Shocked at this*) Well. I suppose that's why you're not teaching Sunday School.

WENDY: Partly. It felt to me like the kids were just paraded up to perform, like a troop of trained seals. They wanted to do a play about the prodigal son. But when the Superintendent saw that they had the prodigal spending his money on drugs, the whole thing got the axe.

DOROTHY: I can see that. *(Awkward pause)* Anyway, Wendy, I'm glad I bumped into you—it will save me a phone call. I'm phoning people for the Fowl Supper, and I've got you down for pies.

WENDY: Pies?

DOROTHY: Three pies. Oh, they can be whatever kind you like, dear.

WENDY: Mrs. Simpson, I don't know how to bake a pie.

DOROTHY: Wendy, then it's time you learned. Your mother was one of the best cooks in town. Why, I remember when she would bring a dozen pies to the Fowl Supper!

WENDY: *(Grimly)* So do I.

DOROTHY: Well, Wendy, the bakery has decent pies. That's what some of the younger women do, you know. Some of them put the bakery pies in their own Tupperware containers, so they don't look store-bought. Others just bring them in the bakery boxes. I suppose it doesn't really matter.

WENDY: You say it as if it does matter.

DOROTHY: Oh, no, just as long as we get the pies. You know, we old ladies aren't getting any younger. We need you young women to start taking over.

WENDY: Taking over? Mrs. Simpson, you ladies won't allow anybody into the church kitchen!

DOROTHY: *(Breezily)* Oh, don't be silly, Wendy. We'd welcome you any time. In fact, we'd love it if you and some of your friends would come to our group meetings. Our group meant so much to your mother.

WENDY: I'll bring you your three pies. What time do you want them?

DOROTHY:	Oh, why not at 5:15, when you come for your shift?
WENDY:	My shift? Mrs. Simpson, I said I'd bring pies. I didn't say I'd work a shift.
DOROTHY:	Well, it is a church supper, dear. Everyone's expected to help out. What sitting are you bringing the family to? I have tickets right here: $7 each for you and Doug, and, let's see…Patty and Andrew and Dylan, that comes to $20.
WENDY:	*(Sighs)* Mrs. Simpson, we're not coming to the supper.
DOROTHY:	What?
WENDY:	We can't afford it. Doug got laid off, and my little job at the library is barely keeping body and soul together. Getting the pies will be hard enough.
DOROTHY:	Well, you know, dear, we've all had hard times. I lived through the depression, I know. But one of the great things about the church is that we can all give of our time. We'll see you at 5:15 for your shift.
WENDY:	Okay, Mrs. Simpson. *(Dorothy exits)* You win. *(Helen enters)*
HELEN:	Hi, Wendy, how are…are you all right? You look like you just got hit by a steamroller. *(Sits)*
WENDY:	Good description.
HELEN:	Hmm. Dorothy?
WENDY:	Yes. Oh, Helen, I know she's a pillar of the church, but…
HELEN:	She's a pillar of a church that doesn't exist anymore.
WENDY:	What do you mean?

HELEN:	Oh, maybe I'm just a crazy old bat who's trying to be with it. I keep telling the girls that times have changed, and they can't expect you young people to do the same things in the same way that we did them forty years ago.
WENDY:	That's exactly what she expects. I have bitterly disappointed her and dishonoured the memory of my dear, departed mother because I'm not teaching Sunday school. She guilted me into bringing three pies for the Fowl Super. And then, she practically spanked me because we can't afford to even eat at the blessed thing!
HELEN:	Oh, dear.
WENDY:	God! She sure pushes my buttons. My mom used to just slave over all those suppers and bazaars. I don't know how she did it. I don't know why she did it. She'd be crabby for days, storming around the house, yelling at us kids. And then we'd have to put on our Sunday best, go to the church, and smile nicely.
HELEN:	You mean the mothers of the past weren't perfect?
WENDY:	*(Laughing)* No more than the mothers of today, I guess.
HELEN:	But despite all the crashing of pots and pans and your mom's grouchiness while cooking up a storm, you're still a part of the church today.
WENDY:	There are other memories, though.
HELEN:	Like?
WENDY:	You know, when Mom went to a church meeting, she'd always come home all fired-up about something or other: missionaries, or outreach to new Canadians, or Bible study. She had such enthusiasm. At the meeting I went to last month, they spent more time talking about the menu for the after-church luncheon than they did in worship.

HELEN: I know. Sometimes we do get carried away over the inconsequential things. You know, sometimes Roger and I do the same thing at home—we spend more time talking about silly stuff than about things that are really important.

WENDY: Yeah, it's the same with Doug and me. But, somehow, I expect the church to be different, to be better than that. I want to be as fired-up as Mom used to get, fired-up about something that matters. You know what I mean?

HELEN: I think so. Sometimes it feels like the church has lost its passion. Almost like we're afraid to struggle for justice anymore.

WENDY: Exactly! I want to be doing something that makes a difference.

HELEN: Me too. Don't get me wrong, friendships are important. And though she drives me crazy sometimes, I wouldn't trade Dorothy in for all the tea in China. But we are a church. We have a purpose and a mission. And a ministry.

WENDY: You sound just like my mom.

HELEN: Wendy, I'm just stepping over to the bakery. Do you have time for a cup of coffee and a cinnamon bun?

WENDY: I'd like that, Helen. I'd like that a lot.

           (They exit)

Bread That Remembers

FROM A STILLNESS WITHOUT SHADOWS

Joseph J. Juknialis

Sermon
Performance time: approximately 20 minutes with congregation's contribution

CHARACTERS:

TREATMENT 1
Narrator/Storyteller
Older Brother
Younger Brother
Wise One
Country Folk—6 or more of all ages

TREATMENT 2
Narrator/Storyteller
Whole Congregation

TREATMENT:

This is a wonderfully rich story for telling and so a storyteller for this would be, for me, ideal. However, it can also be narrated from a podium with good reading skills. (See workshop section of this book.)

In Treatment 1 the narrator or storyteller would have one rehearsal with the two brothers, wise one, and country folk so that they learn their entrance and exit cues. Three of the Country Folk can each be given a line from the story to learn and the order in which the lines will be given.

In Treatment 2 the narrator or storyteller, invite the congregation, before you begin the drama, to remember a time when they personally have been "blessed with life" by someone—perhaps a family member, friend, or a stranger. Ask them to place that experience in a sentence beginning with, "I remember when…" At an appointed time, from where they are seated, they can share their memory as a contribution to the story. Give them a couple of examples of such a sentence. Pre-arrange with someone to start it off at a gesture from you and let this process continue until it feels as though all who wish to speak have spoken. Or cut it off after three to five minutes if you have an uninhibited congregation! Remember to assure them that only those who wish to speak are asked to do so. With this treatment you treat the story as a monologue except for the one section where the congregation joins in.

SETTING:

A table with a loaf of unsliced bread on it placed in the centre of the congregation or on the altar. The action will largely take place around the bread as a focus.

Using this bread for communion or sharing it out at coffee hour provides a powerful addition to the story/drama.

— ◆ —

NARRATOR: A long time ago
                      people had not yet forgotten
                      that bread always remembers
                      what is spoken in its presence.
                      Then everyone knew that if goodness was spoken
                      among those gathered around the bread
                      then those who ate that bread would be blessed;
                      and if it was selfishness and evil that was spoken
                      why then those who ate the bread would be cursed
                      with cold hearts and hardened spirits.

Treatment 1   ***(Enter two brothers who stand or sit facing the
                      congregation.)***

NARRATOR: There were in those days two brothers.
                      Many thought them to be twins
                      for they looked so much alike
                      not only in appearance
                      but also in what they did
                      and how they treated others.
                      However, though they were born in the same year,
                      they were not twins,
                      for the older had been born in January
                      and the younger in December of that very same calendar.
                      Their mother had died in giving birth to the younger,
                      and so the two brothers
                      had been raised by their kind and loving father—
                      each reflecting his goodness and gentleness.
                      Perhaps that is why they were thought to be twins
                      by the many who knew them.

NARRATOR: One day in early spring,
  after they had grown to young manhood,
  yet before either of them had married and left home,
  their father grew seriously ill.
  Before the seeds of that season had sprouted with life
  the father died,
  leaving his sons, then, to depend upon their own goodness.

  (The two brothers stand and turn up stage.)

NARRATOR: Together the two brothers came before the judge of that
  land so that the father's will might be unsealed
  in order that each might receive what the father had
  promised.
  The reading of that will revealed equal portions of life
  for each of the sons.
  Because the father had loved them both,
  without favouritism of any sort,
  each of the sons received half of the farm
  on which he had been raised.

NARRATOR: At this, the elder son grew angry and resentful.
  He had deserved the greater share, he insisted,
  for he was the older of the two;
  and with that he turned away from the judge
  and from his brother
  and left them both
  alone
  in that chamber of justice.

  (Elder brother exits angrily and comes to the table to sit.)

  (Then the younger brother walks slowly off.)

NARRATOR: When the older brother arrived home
  he sat in anger
  at the very table where he and his brother
  together with their father

had shared meals
and love
and life.
There, at that table,
he allowed his anger to unravel more and more. *(Hold one angry pose until exit.)*

NARRATOR: Shattering the gentle stillness which had long been
a family member,
he spewed curses and hatred
at the embarrassed and lonely silence.
Suddenly
he stood, *(stand)*
pounded the table with yet more violence,
and left. *(Elder brother exits very angrily.)*
In all of his anger
what the elder brother had never noticed
was the bread on the table.

(Younger brother enters and sits at table.)

NARRATOR: Shortly thereafter the younger brother came home.
Having found the elder brother gone,
he sat and waited amid the strained silence.
When the older brother never returned
the younger brother ate his evening meal alone *(hold one eating pose for this and the next 3 lines)*
in the torn darkness of that night.
There he ate the bread which had heard the elder's anger,
the bread that remembered.
That night the heart of the younger brother
grew cold and hardened,
scarred with the same selfishness and hatred
which lived within the elder. *(Younger brother exits.)*

NARRATOR: The next day's morning sun
was the sole source of light in the brothers' home.
The older brother did return

but without the gentleness and love which once were his.
So also did the younger brother live
without his father's gifts,
twinned again,
though now in hatred
as once they had been in goodness and peace.

NARRATOR: During those weeks of summer,
the entire countryside came to recognize the change
which had come about between the two brothers.
Their hearts quietly wept in sadness
over that tragic occurrence.

NARRATOR: Somewhere in the middle of that summer
the wise one of the village
invited the inhabitants of the surrounding countryside
to a common meeting.

Treatment 1   *(Wise one enters and stands behind table.)*

NARRATOR: On a warm summer evening
all but the two brothers
came to the village square in the centre of the town.
Men and women gathered;
children tagged along;
strangers were welcomed.

NARRATOR: There, on the table in the centre of their gathering,
was placed a single loaf of bread.
When it seemed that all had arrived,
the one who was wise came before them
and explained why she had called them together.

WISE ONE: If it is true that the bread always remembers, then perhaps we can bring blessings of gentleness and love once again.

NARRATOR: She then invited all those who had come
to tell stories of the goodness

which once lived in the hearts
of both the elder and the younger brother,
and to tell those stories in the presence of the bread—
the bread that always remembers.

Treatment 1   *(Country Folk enter from their pews and stand around the bread.)*

NARRATOR: One by one, then, they came forward
and stood before the bread
and before their neighbours,
there to tell their own story
of how they had been blessed with life
by the two brothers.

NARRATOR: Many stories were told that night,
all in the presence of the bread.

Treatment 2   *(Gesture to the congregation to begin their sharing of stories.)*

Treatment 1

1. "I remember when the brothers took me in when I was sick and lost and a stranger here."

2. "I remember when I broke my leg at the beginning of the planting season and how the brothers worked nights by moonlight to plant my fields after they had planted their own in order that I might have crops to harvest come autumn."

3. "I remember how the brothers shared half their own harvest with me when my barn burned and, with the barn, all of that season's labours as well."

NARRATOR: All evening long villagers and countryfolk
stood in front of everyone
and, in the presence of that lone loaf of bread,
told stories of the gentleness and goodness
which once had made a home among the brothers.
When the last story had been told,
well past the time when many of the children
had fallen asleep

in the arms of their parents,
all those who had gathered
made their way to their homes
and to the healing sleep which awaited them.

Treatment 1   *(Country Folk return to pews.)*

NARRATOR: After all had left
the wise one who had gathered them all
stood alone at the table with the bread.
There, in the summer silence of that night,
she picked up the loaf of bread,
placed it in a sack,
and began her journey to the home of the two brothers.

Treatment 1   *(Wise one picks up loaf and exits down centre aisle.)*

NARRATOR: She arrived just before the sun,
when the nighttime had not yet begun to shed
her skin of darkness.
Her deed was simple
and quickly done—
to leave the bag which held the bread at the door
and depart.

NARRATOR: As she made her way home
amid the early showers of morning sun,
she realized she was not tired
though she had not slept the entire night.
Instead, she felt within herself
a rising hope of life,
fed by the faint possibility
that perhaps the two brothers,
when they found the bread,
might just offer each other that bread
and with it
all of the goodness, gentleness, and love
it remembered.

Journey to Christmas

Louise Smith

Sermon or homily
Performance time: 8 to 10 minutes

CHARACTERS:
Narrator
Nell
Sally

TREATMENT:
This series of scenes is intended to spark thought within the congregation. You may decide to break this play into four separate Sundays during Advent or use it all at once for a Christmas service. The characters should be light as the meaning is rather deep.

SETTING:
You will need a chair in the centre of the chancel. All other set and prop items are mimed except a suitcase and its contents. The suitcase should be filled with dissimilar travel items—like a bathing suit, ski goggles, maps, sun hat, heavy sweater, etc.

— • —

SCENE ONE

NARRATOR: The most important lessons in life are usually the hardest to figure out. These are the lessons that require deep thought. Something similar to a jigsaw puzzle. Either the pieces are huge and fit together easily. Or the pieces number in the thousands and are so tiny and so similar it takes days, even months to fit them into place. Those are the kinds of puzzles that we often give up on. Just like in the journey of life, where we often move forward, before we are ready.

(The scene starts with Sally sitting centre stage, deep in thought. Nell arrives to interrupt Sally's concentration.)

NELL: *(Opening the pretend door to Sally's house and entering.)* Yoo-hoo. Sally, are you here? I'm in the middle of baking chocolate chip cookies. Do you have any chocolate chips I can borrow?

Sally? Sally, are you here? *(Walks in far enough to see Sally deep in thought.)*

SALLY: Oh, sorry Nell. I didn't see you. What was it that you wanted?

NELL: Just some chocolate chips. But Sally, is there something wrong?

SALLY: Why do you ask?

NELL: You seemed so distant. So deep in thought. Is everything okay?

SALLY: Oh heavens yes. Everything is just fine. It's just that…

NELL: What? Just what?

SALLY: I can't explain it. I feel as though I am supposed to be getting ready for something.

NELL: It's a few weeks before Christmas, maybe you're feeling caught in the frenzy.

SALLY: No, no, that's not it. I feel like there is something I should be doing. Something I need to get ready for, but I haven't a clue what it is supposed to be.

NELL: Well friend, *(making a face as though she thinks her friend is losing her noodles)* I'd love to sit around and help you find your way, and all, but the stove is beckoning. Mind if I grab some chocolate chips and hit the road?

SALLY: No, go right ahead. I think I'll sit here and think for a bit longer.

> *(Nell roots in the imaginary kitchen, finds the chips and says goodbye and leaves. Sally sits, deep in thought the whole time.)*

SCENE TWO

(This scene starts with Sally centre stage packing and unpacking a suitcase.)

NELL: *(Same arrival as in first scene.)* Yoo-hoo, Sally, are you home?

SALLY: Uh-huh, come on in, I'm in the living room.

NELL: *(Starting to enter the house.)* Sally, I'm in the middle of making pancakes. Have you any flour and eggs I can borrow? *(Far enough into the house that she sees Sally packing a suitcase.)* Heavens woman! What are you doing?

SALLY: Packing. I think?

NELL: For what? Did you win some trip and forget to tell me? Oh no…are you leaving Bob?

SALLY: No, no, no. I'm getting ready for something.

NELL: What?

SALLY: Well. That's the problem. I'm not sure what I'm getting ready for. I just have this feeling. This funny feeling in my stomach that I am supposed to be doing something. Getting ready for something. *(Picks up a bathing suit.)* And because I haven't the foggiest what this is about, I'm packing everything under the sun. *(Drops in the bathing suit. Then picks up ski goggles and drops them in. Goes through a variety of items that should not be similar.)*

NELL: You are losing it friend. You are really losing it. I'd love to sit around and help you "find" it, but I've got to grab that flour and eggs and be on my way. The kids will be home any minute.

SALLY: Help yourself. I want to finish up with this packing.

(Again, Nell helps herself in the kitchen and lets herself out of the house.)

SCENE THREE

(Sally is sitting centre stage with a closed suitcase in front of her. She seems very excited with anticipation.)

NELL: *(Opening the imaginary door.)* Yoo-hoo, Sally. Are you home? I'm making chicken for supper tonight and I wondered if you have any spare chicken. *(Enters far enough to see Sally sitting with the suitcase.)*

Are you still caught up in that 'packing to be ready' thing?

SALLY: Nope.

NELL: Good. I was beginning to get worried about you.

SALLY: I'm done packing. I'm ready now.

NELL: Ready for what?

SALLY: Still not sure. I've packed everything I could think of and now I'm ready. I am definitely ready for whatever it is that I'm supposed to be ready for.

NELL: *(Walks over and feels her friend's forehead.)* Are you sure you feel okay? Do you want me to call 911? There are very nice doctors at the hospital who know exactly how to deal with these kinds of things. I can call if you like?

SALLY: No, don't call 911. I'm not crazy. I'm just ready. Ready for what life has in store for me next.

NELL: In that case, mind if I just help myself to your chicken? I've got a meal to cook.

SALLY: You go right ahead. I'm going to sit here and wait. *(Acts very excited, like she is about to win the lottery or something.)*

NELL: Promise to call me before you do anything crazy. *(Under breath, to the congregation.)* You can't get any crazier than that. Yikes!

SALLY: I will. I'll see you later Nell.

        (Nell roots through the freezer and lets herself out.)

SCENE FOUR

(This scene starts with Sally centre stage scratching her head like something is wrong. Seated in front of her is the suitcase.)

NELL: *(Enters the imaginary door.)* Yoo-hoo, Sally, are you home? I'm trying to get ready for Christmas dinner tomorrow…

SALLY: Come right in Nell, I've got a spare turkey in the fridge.

NELL: Now how did you know I was going to ask for a turkey? *(Walks in far enough to see Sally scratching her head.)* Sally, you look bothered by something. Everything okay?

SALLY: Well. Sort of. I think I've got this whole packing thing all wrong.

NELL: *(Under her breath—towards the congregation.)* Well, it's about time.

SALLY: Something is not right. *(Opens the suitcase and starts to unpack.)* Something tells me that I won't need all this stuff. I need to be ready, but I don't need to take anything with me. *(With great excitement, starts to throw things out of the suitcase, getting more and more excited with every item that is taken out.)* Yes, this is it. I have to take this all out.

NELL: I can't believe you're making this huge mess, what with Christmas coming tomorrow and all.

SALLY: *(Takes the final item out, and peers into the suitcase.)* That's it. Oh my goodness. That's it. I know what I have been getting ready for.

NELL: Now you have really lost it. *(Peers into the suitcase.)*

Oh. Hmm. Kind of interesting. I think I see what you see. It does kind of look like a manger in there.

(Both peer into the empty suitcase.)

SALLY: You see it too! It does look like a manger. The manger baby Jesus laid in.

NELL: It's just 'cause it's Christmas tomorrow. That's all. It doesn't mean anything more than that.

SALLY: That's where you are wrong my friend. It's more than that. *(Smiling like she just won the lottery.)* Way more than that. I think I know what I've been waiting for. What I've been getting prepared for. *(Sits back down in the chair.)* Go ahead and grab the turkey, Nell, I need to think about this for a while.

(Nell roots through the fridge and lets herself out. Sally remains on centre stage, big smile on her face, deep in thought.)

NARRATOR: And Nell left the house, turkey in hand. Both Nell and Sally had seen the image of a manger inside the empty suitcase. It seemed as though the puzzle was complete, at least for Sally. You see, although Nell saw the image, she saw it with only her eyes. Sally, on the other hand, saw the image not only with her eyes, but with all her heart and soul. Sally was at a point in her life where she finally knew the answer. And Nell. Nell was still unaware of the question.

On Death

Craig Boly

Sermon or homily anytime
Performance time: 5 minutes

CHARACTERS:

Narrator or **Storyteller**
Twin One and **Twin Two**—any age, either or both sexes (just change the
     pronouns in the text).
Or this can be done with **one storyteller**.

TREATMENT AND SETTING:

Narrator takes position to the side or in the pulpit where he or she can see the
twins. The twins can dress in shorts and short sleeves and be barefoot.

    A bench is set in the centre of the chancel with a long cloth stretched out
on the floor in front of the bench. The twins step up to the opposite ends of
the fabric and begin turning inward, holding on to the fabric until they meet
in the middle fully wrapped except for their heads. Together they sit on the
bench and are still with eyes closed. The drama begins.

— ◆ —

NARRATOR:	Once upon a time, life began for twin boys in their mother's womb. The spark of life glowed until it caught fire with the formation of their embryonic brains. With their simple brains came feeling, and with feeling a sense of surroundings, of each other, of self. *(Twins begin to come to life, but keep eyes closed until the end.)* When they perceived the life of each other, they knew that life was good and they laughed and rejoiced, the one saying,
TWIN ONE:	Lucky are we to have been conceived, and to have this world.
NARRATOR:	And the other chiming.
TWIN TWO:	Blessed be the Mother who gave us this life and each other.

NARRATOR: Each budded and grew arms and fingers, lean legs and stubby toes. They stretched their lungs, churned and turned in their new-found world. They explored their world, and in it found the life cord which gave them life from the precious Mother's blood. So they said,

TWIN ONE: How great is the love of the Mother.

TWIN TWO: That she shared all that she has with us.

NARRATOR: And they were pleased and satisfied with their lot. Weeks passed into months, and with the advent of each new month they noticed a change in each other, and they began to see changes in themselves.

TWIN ONE: We are changing. What can it mean?

TWIN TWO: It means, that we are drawing near to birth.

NARRATOR: An unsettling chill crept over the two, and they both feared, for they knew that birth meant leaving all their world behind. Said the one,

TWIN ONE: Were it up to me, I would live here forever.

TWIN TWO: But mightn't there be a life after birth?

TWIN ONE: How can there be life after birth? Do we not shed our life cord and also the blood tissues? And have you ever talked to one who has been born? Has anyone re-entered the womb after birth? No!

NARRATOR: He fell into despair, and in his despair he moaned.

TWIN ONE: If the purpose of conception and all our growth is that it must be ended in birth, then truly our life is absurd.

NARRATOR: Resigned to despair, the one stabbed the darkness with his unseeing eyes, and as he clutched his precious life cord to his chest, he said,

TWIN ONE: If all this is so and life is absurd, then there really can be no Mother.

TWIN TWO: But there is a Mother, who else gave us our nourishment and our world?

TWIN ONE: We get our own nourishment and our world has always been here. And if there is a Mother, where is she? Have you ever seen her? Does she ever talk to you? No! We invented the Mother because it satisfied a need in us. It made us feel secure and happy.

NARRATOR: Thus, while one raved and despaired, the other resigned himself to birth, and placed his trust in the hands of the Mother. Hours ached into days and days fell into weeks and it came time. Both knew their birth was at hand, and both feared what they did not know. As the one was the first to be conceived, so he was the first to be born, the other following after. *(Twins struggle to standing position.)*

NARRATOR: They cried as they were born into the light, and coughed out fluid and gasped in the dry air. And when they were sure they had been born, they opened their eyes for the first time, and found themselves cradled in the warm love of the Mother. They lay open-mouthed, awe-struck before the one they could only hope to know.

> *(Twins open eyes then turn to unwrap themselves letting the fabric drop. They return to standing side by side and face the altar or other sacred symbol in your church. One twin rests head on shoulder of other twin and hold for two beats.)*

— ◆ —

I've often thought this piece, as story or drama, could be a healing sermon at a funeral. For many it gives a helpful new perspective on birth and death.

1 Samuel 1:4–20, 1 Samuel 2:1–10, and Mark 13:1–8 or John 13:31–35 are some examples of scripture that would be appropriate with this drama.

The Pearly Gates

Louise Smith

To begin a sermon or a meeting on inclusiveness
Performance time: 3 minutes

CHARACTERS:
Saint Peter
Man
Woman

TREATMENT AND SETTING:
You could have a table centre stage with a sign over head that reads, "Pearly Gates—entrance exams taken here." Saint Peter could wear a halo and be seated at the table. Or eliminate the table and chair and have Saint Peter, in halo, holding the sign.

— ◆ —

(The couple arrive, arm in arm, entering from the side.)

SAINT PETER: Good morning. You must be the Walshes. I got the message from above that you would be arriving today. I'm so glad to see you made it. Traffic wasn't too bad was it?

MAN: Oh no. We sailed right through.

SAINT PETER: Good. Good. Sometimes, especially around holidays we can be very busy up here. Some are coming, some are going. Oh, sometimes I don't know which end is up.

(Saint Peter stops for a moment and pretends he's hearing someone talk to him from above.)

What's that? Oh yes. You're right. Your way is up. Anyway, back to you two. You must be here to take the test.

WOMAN: I guess. We're not too sure what's happening. We just followed the light and ended up here.

SAINT PETER: Good, good. The light's still shining. That's good to know. I can forward that information to the maintenance crew. Now. The test. Here's the thing. I hand you the sheet of paper. You read the question. You answer the question out loud to me. I grade the answer. Once we get that far, I tell you what happens next. Are you with me?

MAN and WOMAN: Yes, yes, we're with you.

SAINT PETER: Okay, Here's the test. *(Saint Peter hands a paper over to the couple. They read for only two seconds before answering.)*

MAN and WOMAN: Yes. Our answer is yes.

SAINT PETER: *(With much enthusiasm.)* Bingo. We have a winner. You've passed with flying colours. *(Getting up to lead them through the gates.)* Follow me folks. It's this way through the Pearly Gates. You're on your way to heaven. *(Lead couple into front of nave.)*

> *(Through this next part Saint Peter acts as though he is taking the couple on a tour.)*

SAINT PETER: Now folks, I'm gonna have to leave you soon. Before I go, I'll show you the ropes. Seeing you didn't come from any specific group I'm gonna give you the whole tour.

(Pointing) See all these paths. All these paths lead to the same place. Heaven. We usually don't tell people that. We let them figure it out for themselves when they get to the other side. See this path here. This is the path all the Muslims take. And see this path over here. *(Walking a few steps to the side and again pointing.)* This is the path

the Hindus take. And over there, that path is for the Jewish. And this path, it's for those like you who weren't sure. And this path over here. *(Wait a couple of seconds to emphasize the punch line coming up.)* This path you must be very quiet on. *(Again wait a couple of seconds before delivering the punch line.)* This path is for the Christians and they think they're the only ones up here.

Winter

Winter like justice
arrives with our maturing
Incarnational

Elizabeth

A monologue by Betty Radford Turcott

Homily or meditation
Performance time: 3 to 5 minutes

CHARACTERS:

1 **Elizabeth** (In monologue)
Or
2 **Elizabeth** (And one or more **dancers**)

TREATMENT AND SETTING:

In treatment 1 Elizabeth is the storyteller sitting alone on a stool or comfy chair at the top of the chancel steps. She could be dressed as the biblical Elizabeth or in modern dress with shawl. In treatment 2 Elizabeth is the storyteller with a dancer or group of dancers. The action could take place near and around the font if the visibility is good. You could include music, as indicated throughout. This monologue could follow a reading from Luke 1:39–56

— • —

(Elizabeth is seated, wrapped in a shawl. She is quiet, pensive, and serene. She sits remembering and reflecting on her life.)

Treatment 2   *(Dancer(s) in still, resting poses encircling Elizabeth—one could be posed as the olive tree.)*

ELIZABETH: It is pleasant to sit here in my garden. The trees are resting. There are few signs of life, no new leaves, no blossoms, no fruit. The olive tree moans quietly in the winter wind. It seems to be waiting...just waiting. Hmm...I am like that olive tree. My life has its seasons. Seasons of waiting, resting quietly; seasons of growing and of bearing fruit. Seasons of endings and of beginnings.

(Music begins softly and dancers begin to move to the images and themes of the story.)

The days of my youth, were spent longing for the things the future held in store for me. I was happy, and yet there was deep within a need for more. I knew that in God's own good time life would burst forth. And so I waited. As I became older it took strength and courage to hold on to my dream. But all of my life I felt drawn to the mystery of birth and new life. Waiting for the melody I heard in my heart to become music—music swelling and soaring with new life.

(Music and movement continue to reflect the themes of the story—not the literal words.)

I became impatient as the years passed me by. It was hard not to be full of doubt and bitterness. When the monthly sign of my womanhood stopped it was for me a death. The death of dreams, of visions, of fruitfulness. But I learned to let go of my impatience. To let go and to let life be. I became a woman who listened. Listened to the heartbeat of life. And that heartbeat was the sign of faith in tomorrow. I gained the ability to live in the mystery and the wonder. Waiting for spring, like the olive tree in my garden.

The birth of John brought a wonderful symphony to my heart. The child of the promise…the child of my old age…the incarnation of my dreams.

(Dancers return to the original resting/waiting poses.)

And now he has grown and gone. Gone in answer to the music of his own deep mystery. Gone to make new pathways, new roads, new dreams. And I sit in my garden, waiting still; for life, for death, for answers. Waiting for God to reveal the mystery of endings and beginnings.

(Leave a brief silence and then follow this with the prayers of the people.)

Not Just the Pretty Parts

Stephen Bemrose-Fetter

Sermon or scripture and sermon
Performance time: approximately 20 minutes

CHARACTERS:

Ethel—an older woman
Peter—a young man
Abby—a young mother
A life-sized realistic looking **baby doll** or, if you feel courageous,
      a **real baby**.

TREATMENT:

This is a moving, thought-provoking play written in a realistic style. Be sure to allow sufficient rehearsal time to realize its potential.

SETTING:

I suggest reserving the front several pews for a playing area together with the chancel and pulpit. A table and chair should be set up to one side for Ethel. You will need a diaper bag and baby paraphernalia and a manger scene centrally placed.

— • —

(Ethel is working as the narthex volunteer in the church welcoming tourists and other visitors on a grey weekday afternoon shortly before Christmas. Peter bursts in the door and talks in a loud voice, at least to start with. Abby is a regular member of the congregation. She and her baby are already sitting in the empty church, but Peter isn't aware of them until she speaks).

PETER: *(Enters and looks around the front of the nave.)* Wow! It looks like a movie set in here!

ETHEL: *(At her table)* Hello, can I help you?

PETER: It's just like in the movies. Look at that high ceiling, and those lights hanging down. You feel like a squashed ant crawling around on the ground under all that.

ETHEL: *(Walks up to Peter.)* Oh! well…I've never heard anyone describe it that way before. But we're very proud of our church. Now, my name is Ethel, so if you have any questions…

PETER: And those pillars reaching all the way up. And the windows. Awesome! They look so happy in those windows. So bloody self-satisfied. You can really tell they don't know anything about the real world. I bet it makes you all feel really good on a Sunday morning to sit in those pews and listen to all that bull.

ETHEL: *(Nervously)* Well, I do like coming here. Now if you have any questions, I'll just be over at my table.

PETER: *(Derisively)* Yeah! Questions. Right! It's Christmas, and I bet they're all out buying presents for their cute little girls and boys and telling them fairy tales about peace on earth and goodwill. Church never did anything for me.

ETHEL: Oh, I…I'm sorry…

PETER: That there. That's the pulpit where the preacher stands, right? It must feel really good to stand up there and tell all those people where to go. All that carved wood. It must make him look really powerful, like he really knows what he's talking about.

ETHEL: *(Doubtfully, and a little nervously)* Well, we are very proud of our preaching here at _____ Church.

PETER: *(Interrupting, entering the pulpit and turning on the light.)* Cool. Lights and everything. *(In a stained-glass voice.)* All you sinners are going to hell! You hear me!

All that hypocrisy is driving you right to the devil! It's time to repent! Repent! Repent!

ETHEL: O my! That's not exactly the kind of preaching we do here.

PETER: Yeah, well, it's time to tell the truth in here for a change. It's the Word of God, I'm telling you. The flames of eternal damnation are burning away, flickering torches in the eternal darkness, just waiting for you sinners to drop like stones, dragged down by the weight of your sin.

You think you're so full of happiness and light, and you know it's all garbage. The world is full of pain. Pain, that's the real world. You think everything's going all right and then all of a sudden you get your legs cut out from under you and everything falls apart. What are you going to do about that God? Eh? What are you going to do about that?

ETHEL: *(Nervously)* Abby, I think maybe you should get your baby out of here.

PETER: **(Comes down from the pulpit.)** Ah, what's the use? There isn't anybody listening anyway. Just a bunch of fairy tales to make you feel better. Mangers, and stables, and straw. **(Pointing at the manger.)** Is that supposed to be a stable two thousand years ago? Pretty cute if you ask me.

ABBY: *(From pew)* Well, I like that manger up there. It fits with the rest of the place. And I don't know why you have to come in here trashing everything.

PETER: Who are you? Where did you come from?

ABBY: I was here when you came barging in at the door. Don't you have any respect? You ought to be ashamed of yourself.

PETER:	Don't you ever get mad at God? If there is a God. Or is that considered too sacrilegious?
ABBY:	Well I've never come barging into the church spewing hate and filth all over the place.
PETER:	No. I suppose you wouldn't. Too caught up in the whole charade. What did God ever do for you, anyway?
ETHEL:	Sounds like something's really eating you.
PETER:	Yeah, well, I came in here to have it out with God.
ABBY:	That doesn't mean you have to dump it all over the rest of us.
PETER:	I guess I wasn't really thinking about who else might be in here.
ABBY:	You should be a little more considerate before you go shouting and screaming about stuff. Other people have problems too, you know.
ETHEL:	I remember being angry like that when my son Danny was killed by a drunk driver.
PETER:	You?
ABBY:	*(Rise, move to Ethel.)* I didn't know about that, Ethel.
ETHEL:	Well I never went preaching about it from the pulpit.
PETER:	Not quite your style, eh?
ETHEL:	There are other ways to get angry.
PETER:	I can't imagine you getting angry at anything. You look like such a sweet old lady.
ETHEL:	Well, I did. Sweet old ladies have a life too, you know! There were months that went by when I used to come to

church and sit in the pew and just stew about it. I never knew what was going on around me in the service. People would sing and pray and listen to sermons, and I didn't hear any of it. And yet somehow I couldn't just stay away.

PETER: What is it about this place? I mean, I don't believe in God the way you do or anything, but it's impossible to stay angry in here.

ABBY: Isn't that why you came in?

PETER: No, seriously. Is it the architecture or something? The high ceiling? The dim light? There's something about the place that just gives you willies and calms you down at the same time.

ABBY: Now you're starting to sound like I was feeling.

PETER: You feel it too?

ABBY: I love coming in here because it feels like that. But it just isn't working for me today.

PETER: But you were sitting so quietly. I didn't even know you were there. Weren't you praying or something?

ABBY: I was trying to, but I wasn't getting anywhere. Sometimes I can come in here and God feels so close…it's almost as if there were some kind of energy vibrating around the walls and all you have to do is lean out and step into it. But today…I don't know. I don't even know if I believe in God at all today.

PETER: How can you pray if you don't believe in God?

ABBY: How can you be that angry at God if you don't believe in a creator? It's complicated.

PETER: Yeah, I guess so.

ABBY:	It's so busy in the hospital over there, and my father's so sick. Nurses in and out all the time, and doctors, and students, and people taking blood and poking him this way and that. I just…I just needed some quiet before I go back home again. But God's not here today for me.
ETHEL:	*(To Peter)* I don't think you're just angry either. You say you came in here to have it out with God, but you're starting to sound like maybe it would be okay just to talk to God.
PETER:	If God would ever talk back. How can you believe in a God who doesn't answer you?
ABBY:	You're sounding like me again. Ethel, if you felt like that, how come you kept coming to church after your son died?
ETHEL:	It was like I said. I never really quite understood it. But somehow I felt better just being here.
ABBY:	Oh, shoot. The baby needs to be changed, and I left her car seat out in the car. Could you…would you mind…just holding her for a sec while I get the stuff out of the diaper bag?
PETER:	*(Startled and a little scared.)* Oh, you don't want me to hold her. I don't hold babies. My sister-in-law doesn't ever want me to hold her baby.
ABBY:	What's wrong? Afraid of a little baby? Anybody can hold a baby.
ETHEL:	I'll hold her, sweet little thing. Here. Now, there's Mama over there getting things ready.
PETER:	It's not that. I'd love to hold her. It's just that…well, when I told them I was sick Ellen sort of freaked, and

she said that if I ever came near her baby again she'd call the cops and have me thrown out of the house.

ABBY: You're sick? You don't look sick. Is it catching?

PETER: I've got AIDS.

ABBY: *(Relieved)* But that won't hurt the baby! *(Then, embarrassed)* Oh, I mean, I'm sorry you're sick, and all. That's really awful. But AIDS won't hurt the baby.

PETER: I know that. The doctors told me that. But Ellen…Ellen never really understood about Rick, and now I've got AIDS too, and…. Ellen won't even have me in the house any more.

ETHEL: Not much of a Christmas when you can't even hold your new niece—or was it a nephew?

PETER: Niece. Mary-Anna. She's so beautiful.

ETHEL: So you came in here looking for God. No wonder you're so angry.

ABBY: *(Taking the baby.)* Here, Ethel, I'll take her again. Thanks. You don't mind if I change her right here, do you? I've got a changing pad and all.

ETHEL: You go right ahead, dear. A church is about all of life, you know, not just the pretty parts.

> *(Abby goes up to the straw bales by the manger in the chancel and starts to change the baby.)*

PETER: Do you really believe that?

ETHEL: What? That you came in here looking for God? That's why most people come in here.

PETER: No, that a church is about all of life?

ETHEL:	If I didn't I couldn't come here.
PETER:	But I thought a church was…you know, some kind of holy place.
ETHEL:	It is. But for God all life is holy. Even the baby Jesus had to have his diaper changed—or whatever they did back then.
PETER:	Cool. I never thought of it that way before.
ABBY:	I don't think much of your God, if your preaching is any example.
PETER:	Ah, I was just fooling around. I told you that.
ABBY:	No, I mean it. I know that you're really angry, and I guess you've got stuff to be angry about. But do you really think God is so angry all the time?
PETER:	Don't all you Christians think that?…*(Ethel just looks at him. Abby laughs.)* No, I guess you don't.
ETHEL:	I'll bet it was more than just your sister who didn't understand about Rick. I'll bet your getting sick has caused chaos in your family. Is anybody in your family speaking to you these days?
PETER:	How did you know? I…I…
ABBY:	When my Dad first got cancer I was so scared. I imagined all sorts of things about God: That God was angry at him for something. That God was angry at me for not being there. That if only I had been around more, visited more regularly, helped out with things more…
ETHEL:	*(Reassuringly)* New babies can be awfully consuming dear. God knows that.

ABBY: I suppose, but what I'm trying to say is that part of me
          still really wonders whether God did it to hurt me. I
          know it's not what we were taught, and I don't like it. It
          makes me feel all cold and awful inside, but Dad's always
          been so healthy, and strong, and then right out of the
          blue….Then I heard you preaching like some wild-eyed
          TV evangelist and I realized you must think that about
          you too.

PETER: I must think…?

ABBY: That God's so angry with you. That God really wants
          you to burn in hell the way you were talking.

PETER: O come on, I'm not even sure I believe in God, let alone
          in fire and brimstone and all that stuff.

ABBY: I think you believe more than you're letting on. That
          preaching of yours sounded awfully convincing.

ETHEL: You certainly sounded as though you were afraid of
          something. But is it really God you're afraid of?

PETER: Who else would it be?

ETHEL: I can't answer that. But God isn't angry like that. I mean,
          you said it yourself. It's Christmas. How could God do
          Christmas if God is really as angry as all that?

ABBY: It sure doesn't feel like Christmas this year. I don't even
          know if Dad'll live to Christmas. If he does we're going
          to end up with turkey dinner on hospital trays, and he
          probably won't be able to eat any. What kind of Christ-
          mas is that?

ETHEL: *(Leafing through the lectern Bible.)* I just thought of
          something. The minister was talking about it on Sunday,
          but I was only half listening, 'cause it didn't make a lot
          of sense to me then. Now, if I can just find it. *(To herself)*

Let's see, it's Zachariah speaking when John gets named, so it must be before the Christmas story. *(To Abby and Peter)* Oh yes, here it is. Zachariah is John the Baptist's father. And this is what he says John being born means: "Blessed be the Lord God of Israel, for he has looked favourably on his people and redeemed them. He has raised up a mighty Saviour for us in the house of his servant David, as he spoke through the mouth of his holy prophets from of old, that we would be saved from our enemies and from the hand of all who hate us."

PETER: What's that got to do with anything?

ABBY: Don't you see? It's about Jesus. It's about Christmas. Zachariah is saying that John the Baptist is going to be the one to prepare everybody for Jesus' coming, and that when Jesus actually comes he'll be the mighty Saviour who saves us from the hand of all who hate us.

PETER: But what if it's God who's doing the hating?

ETHEL: "He has looked favourably on his people and redeemed them," it says. God doesn't hate. God has to come in Jesus because people hate. Listen. It goes on: "By the tender mercy of our God the dawn from on high will break upon us, to give light to those who sit in darkness and in the shadow of death, to guide our feet into the way of peace." That's Christmas for you.

PETER: It's just a lot of religious mumbo-jumbo. Light breaking on those who sit in darkness. Guiding us into the way of peace. As if it made any difference.

ABBY: I know what you mean. I just wish I could be more sure of it all myself. *(Referring to changing the baby.)* There, that's done. Are you sure you don't want to hold her for a minute? I wouldn't mind, you know.

PETER:	You'd let me hold your baby? You don't know who I am. You don't even know my name.
ABBY:	I know enough to know it's all right. Just come up here and hold her for a minute.
PETER:	She's so beautiful! How can something this small be so beautiful? Look at her tiny fingers.
ETHEL:	She's perfect, Abby. She's just perfect. *(To Peter)* How can you believe in a God who hates when you hold a baby in your arms?
PETER:	Ellen never let me hold Mary-Anna, and you don't even know my name!
ABBY:	What is it?
PETER:	*(Watching the baby)* Hmm?
ABBY:	What is it? Your name?
PETER:	Peter.
ETHEL:	A good name. He didn't always believe either, Peter didn't. But he was one of Jesus' closest friends.
PETER:	So is this what Christmas is about, then, for you? I've always thought it was kind of weird to think of God as a tiny helpless baby but…
ETHEL:	Kind of weird to think of holding the Creator in your arms, and knowing you had the power to hurt God terribly, or to love God to distraction? I still can't hold anybody else's baby without remembering my own. It's hard to imagine God being that small, and still being God.

ABBY: When I hold her I wonder what Mary must have felt. I mean, my baby is special to me, but hers was special to the whole world.

PETER: No, I was being a little more down-to-earth than that. I never thought I would hold a baby again. I can't tell you what it means to be trusted that way. Even just for a few moments. It makes me hope that there's more than fear and hate in the world.

ETHEL: There's more to life than just waiting for your father to die too, Abby.

ABBY: *(Slowly)* I guess if God really was willing to trust us that much, and to come to earth as a tiny little baby like Emily, that's really something. I mean, sure God must get angry sometimes at the terrible things we do to each other, but even when I'm furious with Emily I couldn't ever hurt her. If God cares about us that way, God couldn't ever want to hurt us. Or hate us.

PETER: Yeah. Hate's pretty strong all right. (I ought to know!) But just looking at her makes me feel better. I mean, I'll probably be dead long before she's grown up and yet I got the chance to hold her. To know her just a little.

ABBY: My father'll be dead too, but he keeps saying the same thing. That at least he got to see her. At least he knows that life goes on after he dies.

PETER: That's it, exactly. I always thought life after death meant me living after my death. And I guess it does. But it means this too. It means that we're part of something that's bigger than us; something that carries on even when we have to start playing a different role.

ETHEL: I still get sad at Christmas. I remember when my Danny was a little boy, and all the presents he got. Running

144

around the house on Christmas morning. I still get mad that he had to die in such a stupid accident. But I wouldn't have wanted not to have him. And because of him I think about life so differently.

PETER: I never knew a baby could make such a difference.

ABBY: I think I need to go back to the hospital. I think I'm finally starting to understand why Dad's not so upset about dying.

PETER: Would you like me to help you carry your things to your car on the way out?

ABBY: No, I'll get the diaper bag and stuff. Why don't you bring the baby? Ethel—thank you. I guess God can be around even when it doesn't feel like it.

ETHEL: Merry Christmas, Abby. Merry Christmas, Peter. Come back soon!

(Peter and Abby exit. Ethel returns to her table.)

— ◆ —

A brief silence for reflection would be appropriate before the service resumes.

You may want to hold a discussion following the service on a question such as, "When have I experienced the feelings of one of the characters in this play?"

The Night Lights

Jason Heinmiller

Scripture and sermon on or near Christmas
Performance time: approximately 30 minutes

CHARACTERS:

SPEAKING ROLES:	NON-SPEAKING ROLES:
Narrator (optional)	**Mary**
John Owen-Dad	**Joseph**
Heather Owen-Mom	**Shepherds** (5 or more)
Steve Owen	**Magi** (3 or more)
Owen Children (2)	**Angels** (5 or more)
Little Green Men (2)	**Star Bearer** (or slide of star)*
Gabriel	
Angel	

* A star slide is easily made by cutting a star shape out of the centre of a small piece of card or opaque paper and inserting it into an empty slide frame.

TREATMENT:

If this is being done at night make sure you have ample light adding spots, where necessary, on all the playing areas.

The contrast of putting the Modern Family in modern clothes, (with the children in pajamas), and the nativity characters in biblical dress is the most effective. You can let your imaginations go wild for the aliens. Clown costume patterns are readily available and could be made in bright green. Such a baggy, one piece outfit will fit easily over angel gowns for the surprise ending costume change.

As an alternative to a balcony the Modern Family could be on a platform at the foot of the chancel steps or down stage in the chancel. The nativity scenes would be in the centre aisle and then move through the centre of the Modern Family's "living room" to assemble up stage as a tableau. This, in fact, provides a nice connection to the story.

If you cannot find the large cast required for this play, an alternative would be to replace the nativity characters with a nativity scene. The narrator is optional as the drama flows quite nicely without this role.

If only the first verse of the carols, included in the drama, is sung the congregation can join in without books and without house lights which would interrupt the drama. Of course other carols or music can be substituted for the ones indicated in the script.

SETTING:

Three playing areas:

1. An area with chairs for the **Modern Family** (could be a balcony or an alcove, where they can be seen by everyone).

2. An area for the **shepherd's** and **angel's scene** (centre aisle or cross aisle or bottom of chancel steps).

3. A focus area where the **nativity tableau** can assemble (in chancel around altar).

— • —

SCENE ONE

(House lights down. Spot up. Enter Narrator.)

NARRATOR: It is Christmas Eve, and the children are gathered around their father, who is reading *The Night Before Christmas* to them.

(Exit Narrator. Spot Down.)

DAD: "And I heard him exclaim as he rode out of sight. Merry Christmas to all and to all a good night." The End.

MOM: All right guys, time for bed; the story is over. We've got a big day ahead of us tomorrow.

KID #2: But I'm not tired; I don't want to go to bed.

DAD: You're going to need your rest.

KID #1: Why can't we stay home tomorrow?

MOM: Because I said so.

KID #2: Read us another story Dad.

DAD: It's nine o'clock. We've already let you stay up later than usual.

MOM: The faster you get to sleep, the faster morning will come.

DAD: That means the faster you can open your presents.

MOM: Besides, *(tries to shoo them off to bed)*, Santa Claus won't come if you're not in bed asleep.

KID #1:   Santa never comes anyway. He's not real.

DAD: I don't think old St. Nick would be pleased to hear you talking like that.

MOM: Shh…*(pause)* I think I hear him on the roof.

KID #2:   *(Walks a step or two, turns to Kid#1.)* Come on, we won't get any presents if we're not asleep.

KID #1:   Don't be a baby…

STEVE: *(Off)* Ho, Ho, Ho, Merry Christmas. I hope everyone is asleep. I'm about to come down the chimney.

(Kids race offstage. Enter Steve.)

DAD: How the heck are ya, Stevie?

STEVE: You always leave your door unlocked?

DAD: *(Jokes)* This isn't Winnipeg *(or _____)*. We don't have to watch our backs all the time out here.

STEVE: *(Chuckle)* It ain't that bad out there. What'd you think of the Santa bit. Did I fool the kids?

DAD: Oh ya, perfect timing. You should have seen their faces…

MOM: And how quick they ran off. How was your trip?

STEVE: Long and boring, Heather. I can't stand driving through the prairies *(or _____)*. You know I almost fell asleep at the wheel this year. That's what happens when you drive for long periods of time. You start to doze off and next

thing you know you're in the ditch, or worse, in someone else's lane.

DAD: I still think you should move back here with the rest of
the family.

STEVE: I know John; but, I'm really busy right now. I could
barely find the time to make it out here. Maybe someday
I will.

MOM: Well, it's good that you're here for the holidays. The kids
will be happy to see their uncle in the morning. Can I get
you some eggnog?

STEVE: All right, pour me a glass. You know, every year you
guys want me to come home at this time. It's cold. It's
windy. There's ice on the road. What's so important
about Christmas, anyway? Why can't I come home in
the summer?

DAD: Let's not talk about this now, Steve. Why don't you have
a seat. We were just about to watch a Christmas special
on WGN *(or_____).*

 *(Steve and John sit, mime turning on TV. Mom gives
 each a glass of eggnog, sits, opens a book.)*

STEVE: Isn't there a hockey game or something on?

 *(Mom snaps book shut and sends a sharp look to
 Steve.)*

STEVE: Oops. *(Pause)* Tradition?

DAD: Huh? *(Pause)* Oh, kinda.

 (Freeze scene. Spot up. Enter Narrator.)

NARRATOR: Same old story. Heather and John have trouble getting
the kids to bed. It's late and they have relatives to visit in
the morning. After the children go to bed, Mr. and Mrs.

Owen can finally sit down and rest. Their free time this day is interrupted however, on a good note, by John's brother Steve, who made the trip to _____ from _____ for the holidays. Although Steve doesn't bring any Christmas spirit with him, the Owens are happy to see him nonetheless. This is the first time in a few years he has been home for Christmas. But that's not the only thing special that would happen this night...

*(**Theme of** Twilight Zone **is played. Actors look around confused. Music stops. Resume play.**)*

Scene Two

> *(Exit Narrator. Spot down. Slow flashes of light begin outside the house.)*

MOM: *(Notices lights. Walks to window.)* John look at this. *(No answer.)* John! *(Turns to him.)* What is it?

> *(Steve and John walk to window.)*

DAD: I don't know. *(Jokes)* Maybe Santa's little elves got lost and the lights are a search party.

MOM: Funny, very funny. I want to know what it is.

STEVE: Well, there's only one way to find out. *(Throws John a coat.)* Come on, let's take a look.

MOM: I think I'll stay here. *(Sits down)*

DAD: Suit yourself. We won't be long. Five, ten minutes tops.

> *(Steve and John exit through doorway. Walk toward lights. Enter two comical-looking aliens. Flashing lights stop. Steve and John see the little green men, race back to house. Aliens slowly follow. Steve locks door. He and John sit.)*

MOM: Is everything taken care of? *(No answer.)* What happened out there?

STEVE: Nothing. It's just lightning. Let's watch TV. *(Steve flips channel)*

DAD: Hey, turn it back!

MOM: Honey?

DAD: What is it?

MOM: The lights?

DAD: Don't worry about it. Let's enjoy the rest of the evening.

(Aliens knock at door in mime.)

MOM: *(Pause)* Are you going to answer the door?

STEVE: No. *(Pause)* Whoever it is will come back another time.

MOM: What is going on? *(Walks to door.)*

DAD: *(Trying to sound calm.)* Don't answer it; if we wait, they'll go away.

MOM: *(Unlocks door and places hand on doorknob.)* Stop being so paranoid, It's Christmas. It's not like a bunch of little green men are out there knocking at our door.

(Mom opens door, gasps, jumps back. Steve and John move toward far "wall.")

ALIEN #1:   Relax humans. It was not our intent to frighten you. On this night we have been sent for information.

ALIEN #2:   We are from out there, (points to window), and have come to research your winter traditions.

STEVE: What?!

ALIEN #2:   All we ask is for you to explain this Christmas season to us. We will then be on our way and you will not hear from us again.

STEVE: You've got to be kidding.

ALIEN #1:   Sir, we do not joke. This is a serious mission that we are on.

MOM: Would you excuse us for just a second?

ALIEN #1:   Why certainly.

(Mom moves to be with others. The conversation is not heard by the aliens.)

STEVE: This…ah…um…this can't be happening.

MOM: Listen, they just want some information. If we go along with them, I think they'll leave quicker.

DAD: I don't think we have a choice.

STEVE: *(Sarcastic)* We never have this kind of stuff happen to us in _____!

DAD: What! You think this happens every day?

MOM: Quiet, this is no time to argue. *(To Steve)* How much do you know about the Christmas story?

STEVE: No problem. See, it was so stormy that night, Santa Claus needed Rudolph's glowing nose to guide him.

MOM: I meant the Bible's Christmas story.

STEVE: Oh, *(pause)* not much.

DAD: I think we can get by.

MOM: I hope so. I guess it's settled. *(To aliens)* Have a seat, and we'll get started.

(All sit. Alien #2 takes notes during Scene 3.)

SCENE THREE

(Mary enters biblical playing area—Gabriel appears in pulpit or enters and moves to Mary.)

MOM: Where to begin, where to begin? Well I guess it all started in a place called Nazareth. In that small town lived a woman named Mary, who was soon to be married. One night an angel named Gabriel appeared to Mary and told her of the future. Gabriel explained to Mary that she would give birth to a son, who would be the Saviour of the world. This was indeed odd, because Mary was a virgin.

ALIEN #1:   Virgin? We are not familiar with the word.

MOM: Well a virgin is a person who has never…ah…well, that is…

DAD: What my wife means is…*(pause).* Do you know how children are made?

ALIEN #2:   Yes, first the male…

DAD: Ya, ya, okay. Well Mary never did that.

(Spot up on Mary and Gabriel.)

GABRIEL: Do not be afraid, Mary, for you have found favour with God. And now, you will bear a son, and you will name him Jesus. He will be great, and the Lord God will give to him the throne of his ancestor, David.

ALIEN #2:   If Mary was a virgin, how could she be pregnant?

STEVE: I can't believe you guys are doing this!

DAD: *(To Steve)* If you aren't going to help us then keep quiet. *(To aliens)* Well it's a miracle. We have to accept that it happened. Anyway, Gabriel did not only speak with

Mary, but also with her future husband, a carpenter named Joseph. *(Joseph enters biblical playing area.)*

(Gabriel walks to Joseph. Spot follows.)

GABRIEL: Joseph, son of David, do not be afraid to take Mary as your wife for the child conceived in her is from the Holy Spirit. She will bear a son, and you are to name him Jesus, for he will save his people from their sins.

STEVE: How can you guys remember all that? I haven't heard that story since Sunday school, and that was decades ago!

DAD: *(Ignores him)* Okay, back then the president or something, said everyone had to go to their ancestors' home town, for taxes. Joseph was a relative of David, so he and Mary went to Bethlehem. They looked all over, but every motel was full. Luckily, a kind innkeeper offered his stable for the night. With nowhere else to go, Mary and Joseph slept that night in a barn.

(Hymn: O Little Town of Bethlehem)

(Mary, Joseph, and Gabriel walk through the modern playing area and off stage to receive baby then proceed to bench in centre of chancel while hymn is sung. Star appears held by Star Bearer or a slide of a star is projected on the up stage wall.)

STEVE: Ya, and wasn't the kid born there too?

(Shepherds enter at back with one angel.)

MOM: *(Disgusted)* The kid? Jesus was born there. And Mary laid her child in a manger to sleep. Meanwhile, on the outskirts of town, shepherds were looking after their sheep…

STEVE: And one got lost, so the shepherds left the others behind, and went looking for it.

MOM: No. Wrong story. Then an angel appeared to them.

(Spot up on shepherds and angel.)

ANGEL: Fear not: For, behold, I bring you tidings of great joy. For unto you born this day in the city of David, a Saviour, which is Christ the Lord. Ye shall find the babe wrapped in swaddling clothes, lying in a manger.

(Enter other angels at back.)

MOM: Then a multitude of angels appeared and sang praises to God.

OTHER ANGELS: Glory to God in the highest, and on Earth peace and good will toward all.

(This could be sung by choir or a single voice while the angels do a simple circular dance around the shepherds.)

STEVE: So they never did find the lost sheep?

DAD: There was no lost sheep!

SHEPHERD: Let's go to Bethlehem and see what the Lord has told us about.

(Various shepherds can add improvisational lines ending with this line as a cue.)

STEVE: Oh ya, I remember. They went to the stable and worshipped him.

(Hymn: Angels From the Realms of Glory)

(All walk through modern living room to assemble in stage picture with Holy Family while hymn is sung.)

DAD: Then did the Wise Men come and give Jesus their money?

MOM: Well the Wise Men didn't come right away. It wasn't until a couple of years later they showed up. You see, they were astrologers. They studied the stars. At the same time Jesus was born, a new star appeared in the sky. Amazed, they followed it to the house where Jesus lived.

ALIEN #1:   House? I thought you said they stayed in a stable?

DAD: The star appeared when Jesus was in the stable, but you have to give the Wise Men time to travel. When they found Jesus, the family was living in a house.

STEVE: *(Not quite sure.)* The Magi, it is Magi, isn't it?

DAD: Yup, go on.

STEVE: Well, they brought gold, frankincense, and myrrh as gifts for him.

MOM: Yes! Good for you!

            (Enter Magi at back.)

MAGI #1:   Where is the child born to be king of the Jews? We saw his star in the east and have come to worship him.

            (This line could be divided among two or three Magi and/or improvisation could be added with this line last as cue.)

            (Hymn: We Three Kings)

            (Magi walk through modern living room to join the Holy Family stage picture while hymn is sung.)

MOM: This baby Jesus, would grow up and save the world from its sins. He was nailed to a cross on Calvary—he suffered, so we wouldn't have to. And that's why we celebrate his birthday, every 25th of December.

            (Aliens rise, Alien #1 walks to door.)

ALIEN #1:   Thank you humans, this will help our leader a great deal.

ALIEN #2:	*(To Alien #1)* Not so fast. Let us first see if we have the story straight. *(To humans)* A long time ago in Bethlehem, there was a child born in a stable. His mother was a virgin, and his father was a carpenter.
MOM:	Almost. Jesus' father was God. Joseph, the carpenter, just took care of him on Earth.
	(Alien #2 makes note.)
ALIEN #2:	When the baby was born, a bright star appeared in the sky, and shepherds came to see the child.
ALIEN #1:	Then later on, Wise Guys showed up.
STEVE:	Wise Men.
	(Alien #2 makes note.)
ALIEN #1:	They gave the child expensive gifts.
ALIEN #2:	And Jesus was crucified, so the world might be spared destruction.
STEVE:	Yup. You got it.
	(Aliens walk out door.)
ALIEN #1:	Goodbye humans, thank you.
MOM:	Good-bye.
DAD:	See ya.
STEVE:	Later.
	(Aliens proceed to exit the way they came. Mom and Dad sit. Spot up. Enter Narrator.)
NARRATOR:	The encounter left Heather and John with a reassurance of their knowledge of the Christmas story. And it left Steve a new perspective on the Christmas season.

STEVE: *(Soliloquy)* It's not only the trees and lights that make Christmas special. Those are just material things. It's not about presents or cold icy winds. Christmas is about remembering the story of Jesus' birth, and what that means to us. It's about being together with family and friends, celebrating the birth of our Saviour.

(Scene in living room freezes. Spot up on aliens.)

ALIEN #1: *(Look back at house.)* I was wrong. The story hasn't been forgotten. The Lord will be pleased.

(Aliens remove costumes to reveal themselves as angels. Hold two beats and then join other angels in stage picture. All hold two beats as tableau.)

(Hymn: Joy To The World)

(Biblical characters move out of tableau and down centre aisle to their pews led by Holy Family and angels with Modern Family at the rear while hymn is sung. Stage lights down.)

Bethlehem Cafe

Matthew Penny

Christmas homily or sermon
Performance time: 10 to 12 minutes

CHARACTERS:
Narrator
Betty
Joe
Mary
Shepherd
Larry Wise
Tom Wise
Phyllis Wise (needs reasonable singing voice)
Infant

TREATMENT AND SETTING:
You would need one set in a clearly visible space. An altar/communion table with a checkered cloth would be a nice symbolic table for the guests of the cafe to sit around on high stools. The "doorway" could simply be the chancel steps with the characters making their entrances from the nave aisles. Christmas lights in the cafe would enhance the setting. Appropriate modern costumes seem best with coats for all but Betty. The **Narrator** might dress in biblical garb for contrast and historical perspective.

PROPS:
cups or mugs for all
sheepskin seat cover (probably carried in a bag)
large road map (**Wise People** might carry brief cases)
large CLOSED sign
cloth for Betty to clean off table
Joe might carry a suitcase or back pack and remove a baby bottle from it to feed the babe.

(The scene opens with the cafe owner cleaning off tables and humming a Christmas Carol to herself. The sign at the back of the cafe says, "closed" and it looks as though the day's work is over.)

NARRATOR: Christmas Eve at the Bethlehem Cafe, and the world slows down once more for that one day that seems so unlike all the others. This year, like all the others, Betty is tidying up and getting ready for a quiet day at home. It's been a long day, as usual and she is tired and willing to go home anytime, when...*(There is loud, insistant knocking at the door.)*

BETTY: Now who can that be? *(Loudly)* We're closed, it's Christmas Eve *(Mutters)* Don't go away mad, just go away! *(Loud knocking again, and Betty goes to the door and opens it allowing a young and rather unkempt couple to enter.)*

BETTY: *(sounding irritated)* Okay, it's Christmas Eve and I'm trying to get home, what can I do for you?

JOE: *(desperation in his voice)* Hi, I know it's late, but you see we've been travelling and there isn't anywhere to stay. We just wanted to get home for the holidays and Mary my wife here has a new baby. Cute eh? And the car broke down and it's snowing and we've no place to stay and we just wanted a cup of coffee and wondered if, well...that is...maybe.

BETTY: Now I'm not used to charity cases here. I run a small little diner and barely make a living. I just want to get home, sit down with a drink, and have a quiet time. I'm closed two days a year—Christmas Day and New Year's Eve. This is my holiday and the last thing I need is a couple of wandering kids to bug me.

(Mary begins to cry softly and closely cuddles the baby that she has been quietly holding in her arms.

The other two stare at her and you can feel Betty's heart melt.)

BETTY: Now, now dear, just sit down and relax, I know you must be tired, I remember having kids, they were…*(Guides Mary to a table and a chair, and stops in her tracks when she sees the child.)* How old is this baby anyway? He looks brand new.

MARY: He was just born. They don't keep you in the hospital long these days I guess.

BETTY: *(Betty is shocked and moves in like a mother hen.)* Saints preserve us. Now dear you just sit right here and I'll get you something hot. A mom's got to keep herself healthy if she's going to take care of a little one so new as this. Just you relax and *(to Joe)* You give me a hand…

NARRATOR: And there were in that district shepherds keeping watch over their flocks by night, and an angel of the Lord.

(Betty and Joe bustle about getting a cup for Mary and continuing to do things in preparation for feeding and such. There is only a short pause before there is another knock at the door.)

BETTY: *(mutters)* Now what…*(loudly)* Who is it? It's Christmas Eve and we're closed…*(The knocking continues and is loud and insistent.)* Okay come in then, but beware I'm not in a good mood.

SHEPHERD: Hi, I'm sorry to bother you, but I was driving home for the weekend and got really sleepy. I usually work nights but have a holiday off. Boy it sure is snowing out there. Is there a cup of coffee left in the pot, lady? My friend Harold Angel said if I ever came to Bethlehem that this cafe was the place to be, that something special would happen here. You wouldn't send away a traveller on Christmas Eve would you?

BETTY: You don't know me very well, do you bud? I just told these two that I'm on my way home for a quiet Christmas off. The cafe is closed!

SHEPHERD: Oh, but I see they…What a beautiful baby. Is he yours? Well yes of course he is. I see what Harold meant by that line. (*Moves in and looks at the child carefully; he is obviously amazed by what he sees.*) I've never seen a child that is so,…so…special. My, my….

BETTY: (*sighs heavily*) Well, you might as well come in. Joe, get the man a coffee and then maybe we can all be on our way. I'm going to turn off the decorations and get out of here before the whole world shows up.

JOE: (*to Shepherd*) Well, here you go, (*jokingly with a slight French accent*) I'm not your usual waiter sir, the staff you know want the holiday off, but if you will be seated here, I'm sure that we can be of service to you this evening. (*They both laugh.*)

SHEPHERD: You do that very well. Is this your usual line of work?

JOE: Oh no, I'm a cabinet maker, the best little woodshop in Nazareth you know. Mary and I just had a baby and we were going to my home town for Christmas to…well, sort of pay our dues with the family, if you know what I mean.

SHEPHERD: Oh I sure do. I'm in wool myself. I actually sell sheep-skins, you know, the kind they use in beds, and on seat covers, and such. A young mother might like to have one in her rocking chair. They are really comfortable.

JOE: Oh, I don't know, we've had a difficult year and with the baby…(*trails off*)

BETTY: Okay, everybody drink up, it's getting awfully late, and "Mr. Bean's Christmas" (*or* _____) will be on TV in a few minutes, I don't intend to miss it.

> *(There is a sudden amount of noise in the background and three people enter from the back. They are obviously lost and are messing around with a road map. There is no knocking, just the stomping of feet as they come in, stand at the back, and look around the cafe.)*

LARRY WISE: Hello everyone, how's it going for you this Christmas? We've come a long way and I'm not sure if we're there yet or not. *(The others all respond with a hello or hi, or how's it goin' eh.)*

BETTY: Listen guys, I don't want to seem rude or anything, but is there something we can do for you. It's past closing, Christmas Eve, and we're just sort of about to leave. Can we help you with something?

TOM WISE: We saw the lights were on, and we are like insects in the night attracted to the brilliant illumination and the wonderful star hanging outside the cafe. It seemed like a welcoming if not unlikely spot to rest for a few minutes from our busy travels towards the ultimate destination of love and peace.

JOE: What did he say?

SHEPHERD: I don't know, but it sure sounded nice didn't it? Say guys did you see that the young woman has a baby. He sure is special. Take a look. *(Mary glances at Shepherd then shows the baby to the three who have just entered.)*

PHYLLIS WISE: What a wonderful child. This is a sign for everyone. In the midst of a cruel and dark world, new life is given in a child like this. *(Begins to hum or sing "What Child Is This" or other suitable song.)*

BETTY: Who are you guys anyway?

TOM WISE: I'm Tom Wise, and these are my colleagues in computing Larry and Phyllis. We work for Microsoft building astronomy software for universities. We can find you any planet in the sky but I'm afraid Phyllis can't find anything even with a road map.

PHYLLIS WISE: But what a wonderful child. She is adorable.

MARY: He.

PHYLLIS WISE: A brand new he. Wonderful. This child needs a gift on Christmas Eve. Now Tom, Larry, what can we give this wonderful child? *(They sputter and stammer.)*

SHEPHERD: Well, I sell sheepskins for the benefit of those who need softness and comfort. And on this day I'd be glad to...

PHYLLIS WISE: *(Interrupts him quickly.)* Why thank you...What a wonderful gift. *(Takes the sheepskin and gives it to Mary who puts it under the baby Jesus.)*

SHEPHERD: Well what I meant was...

LARRY WISE: Now I'm not sure, but something tells me this child should have a star named after him, that would be a nice gift too. It would mean he would last forever.

MARY: Thank you so much. You all have been so kind. I just know that there is something special about our new son.

BETTY: You are right, Now everyone sit down and we'll have a hot drink. If you are lucky there may be some pie in the cooler and I know there's lots of fruitcake. Don't worry, Mary. There's a little apartment upstairs. You and Joe and the baby can stay there tonight. Everyone body else it seems has somewhere to go. But just for now let's celebrate.

(Everyone raises their glasses/mugs in a toast, then they all sit.)

NARRATOR: It came to pass that Mary, bore her child. He was not born in a house and there was no room in the place where they went for rest. An Angel appeared to shepherds nearby and called them to come see this great thing that had happened. They came and were amazed by the child. Soon after this, wise people arrived from the East following the light of a new star and brought gifts to the child. And all were amazed by this child and Mary kept these things and pondered them in her heart. And the world was never the same again. The story has been told and retold throughout history. It is one of hearts that were cold being warmed. It is the story of a small child bringing great hope to a dark night and a whole world. It is the story of God's love being so great that nothing at all could keep the love of God from the world.

(The cast could exit down the centre aisle slowly allowing everyone to have a close look at the baby while wishing individuals and all a happy Christmas.)

Christmas Proclamation at Midnight

Kelly Walker

Call to worship or opening rite
Performance time: 6 or 7 minutes

CHARACTERS:

1. **One strong Proclaimer** alone or with four other readers at the end (perhaps choir members).
or
2. **The Proclaimer(s)** and **traditional costumed nativity characters** (real baby, if possible).
or
3. **The Proclaimer(s)** with **traditional nativity characters** plus symbols of the elements mentioned in the text.

TREATMENT:

This can be done quite effectively with one good reader alone, proclaiming the poetic text from the front. I suggest it be done exclusively in candlelight and read slowly to allow the listeners time to call forth the many images in their imaginations.

If you elect to do this with a full cast, invite the congregation, ahead of time, to bring in framed photos of family members, friends, animals, any living thing that was loved and has died.

SETTING:

Bench set in front of altar or in centre of chancel. Use length of centre aisle and centre of chancel as playing area (if done with a full cast).

Proclaimer moves from the entrance or back of church up centre aisle while speaking (if reading, mount script in folder or book for dignified appearance). Other players enter the chancel from their various pews through out the nave.

— • —

PROCLAIMER: Come all of you who wander weary in this world
a world once crowned in splendour
once bathed in radiant harmony
a world that danced as one with all the forces of creation.
Come all of you who search for meaning
in a world where noise is king
where dreams have lost their radiance
where treasures forged in plastic dominate.
Come all of you who yearn for love
in a world where people
bomb the breath of living from their lives
who arm themselves to kill their own kind
who forfeit harmony for hate.
Come all of you who still have hope
for new tomorrows of truest food
to fill our starving bodies and our souls.
Come all of you who hope for shelter from the storm
who dream of dancing a new dance
on a festive night like this.

(Arrives at top of chancel step and turns.)

O come now and please rejoice with me
for in our midst has come the promised one of old
the new Adam, the David for this age,
Jesus, Emmanuel, the friend for humankind.

(Christ candle is lit.)

For on this night is born in hope
the festive dream come true
the one who breaks the darkness of our sorrows and
our fears.

Treatment 2 and 3   *(Holy Family enters and sits on bench in chancel.)*

The breath of God, the smile of joy,
the face of one we've only dreamed we'd see.
In Bethlehem, the house of bread
is born the food of unity and peace.

168

(Angels, and any other airborne creatures, enter chancel and assemble around the Holy Family.)

This blessed night I call on all the angels,
all the birds and all the airborne craft
to congregate in joy and sing their praises to the heights.

Treatment 3   *(An adult and child enter, in modern cloths, with the congregation's framed photos of those who have died and arrange them where they can be seen in the nativity stage picture.)*

I call on all the creatures we no longer see,
our mothers and our fathers long forgotten to us all.
I call on creatures who dance within our earth,
you plants and rocks and animals
to bless this holy night.

Treatment 3   *(Enter two others with plants and rocks that have been provided by congregants.)*

I call on all you swimming creatures
who undergird this earth.
O wondrous friends of water
come and wonder at this night.

Treatment 3   *(Still others enter with sea shells and perhaps a fish in a fish bowl.)*

For unto us a child is born, the son of Mary,
the very dream of God,
the word who breaks the silence of despair.
Rejoice with me and pray that once again this year, the
tent of God
be pitched with us,
the love of God
unfolded,
the hope of all the ages be enfleshed in all our lives.

PROCLAIMER: Radiant child

READER 1:   Prince of peace

READER 2:   Mighty lover

READER 3:   Herald of truth

READER 4:   Dream fulfilled

READER 1:   Wondrous mystery

READER 2:   Thrilling story

READER 3:   Morning star

READER 4:   Glory of God

PROCLAIMER: Be here among us.

> *(Lights up. Christmas carol sung by whole congregation while Holy Family, angels and others return to their pews leaving symbols of life there for remainder of service.)*

Blind Expectation

Jessica Booker

Homily or sermon at Christmas or Epiphany time. Could be preceded by a reading of the story of the slaying of the holy innocents.
Performance Time:
Treatment 1—12 minutes; Treatment 2—14 to 15 minutes

CHARACTERS:

TREATMENT 1 (small cast)	TREATMENT 2 (larger cast)
Prophet / Narrator / Magi / Scribes	**Prophet**
Herod	**Herod**
Asa	**Asa**
Hecklers (planted in audience)	**Hecklers** (planted in audience)
	Narrator
	Mary, Joseph, and **Baby**
	Three Magi
	Scribes and **Priests** (any number)

TREATMENT AND SETTING:

Actors will find the technique of high and low status (see workshop chapter) particularly useful in this play.

TREATMENT 1

Herod and **Asa** in dialogue with each other and with the audience at the top of the chancel step or other visible spot. A **Narrator** would take the lines of the **Prophet, Narrator, Magi,** and **Scribes**. Plant **Hecklers** in the audience. Biblical costume is indicated for this play as written, however, this play echos many political situations of today and modern dress might help make that point. No set or props are needed.

TREATMENT 2

Preset a bench up stage for **Mary, Joseph** and the **Baby** to sit on at the appropriate time and add anything else to enhance a nativity setting. Increase the characters by casting the **Prophet, Narrator, Magi, Scribes,** and, of course, the three non-speaking **Holy Family** roles separately.

— ◆ —

PROPHET: *(in pulpit or to the side or back of nave)* Behold, a virgin shall be with child, and will bring forth a son, and they shall call his name Emmanuel, which being interpreted is, "God with us."

(Enter Herod, King of Judaea)

HEROD: *(to audience—in high status)* Familiar words: Holy scripture. The prophesies of God! Panacia of the poor! My people, Israel, lived for generations in the expectation of a deliverer, a holy Messiah, sent from God. I, Herod, reasoned thusly: if it kept them happy to live in this state of anticipation, and it cost me nothing personally, then I had no objection. That's good politics!

(Enter Asa, advisor to Herod. He is agitated.)

ASA: *(loud whisper—in low status)* Sir, a word with you, I beg.

HEROD: Not now, Asa. Can't you see I am speaking with these good people? *(indicates audience)*

ASA: *(wringing hands)* As your legal advisor, sir, I really must object. Say no more!

HEROD: The time for caution is past. I shall speak. Good evening, my dear friends. You see before you the one who was called Herod, King of Judaea.

HECKLERS: *(loudly)* Boo! Boo! *(repeated several times)*

ASA: I warned you!

HEROD: *(to audience)* Now, wait a minute. Let's get something straight. I was not the Herod who was responsible for the death of that hippy prophet, John the Baptist. That happened at the hands of another Herod years after my death. *(to Asa)* Tell them. Was I not known far and wide as Herod the Great?

ASA: You were indeed, sir.

HEROD: And who bestowed that title on me?

ASA: Why your own people, the Israelites!

HEROD: They loved me.

ASA: That's not quite accurate, sir. *(Herod scowls.)* Let's just say that they were grateful.

HEROD: *(indignant)* Grateful? I should think they would be! How many rulers are also talented architects? Well, I was! *(to audience)* I designed and built many beautiful structures in Jerusalem during my reign. It was through my efforts that the Temple of Solomon rose again grander than ever before. I never lived to see its completion, but I was the planner of that glorious edifice. History cannot take that away from me!

HECKLER: Murderer!

PROPHET: In Rama was there a voice heard, lamentation, and weeping, and great mourning, Rachel weeping for her children, and would not be comforted, because they are not.

ASA: Sir, you must know that you are addressing a hostile audience. What is the point? Let sleeping dogs lie, I say.

HEROD: *(sarcastic)* do you, indeed? Well, I say that I am weary of being remembered only as a slayer of children. Decisions must be made. For every political decision, there is a reason. And I had mine.

ASA: But you were a king! Kings are not responsible to anyone! I just do not see what purpose it will serve to rehash old history.

HEROD: *(gestures to audience, angry)* Look at them out there, passing judgement on me! I insist they understand the pressure I was under at that time.

ASA: *(sigh and raise status)* Very well. If you are determined to explain your actions, then so be it. Will you allow me to set the stage for you?

HEROD: *(petulantly)* Oh, very welll. Get on with it.

ASA: *(to the audience, moving away from Herod)* We were living in turbulent times. The mighty eagle of Rome had spread its powerful wings over our little country. My master, Herod, had the thankless task of satisfying both sides. He was the consummate politician, walking the political tightrope with shrewd cunning.

HEROD: It was not the time for the faint of heart. Subtlety and honeyed promises worked well for me.

ASA: Cyrenius was governor of Syria then, and Herod entertained him lavishly, pleasing Caesar, while, at the same time, seeking approval from the Jews with the restoration of Solomon's Temple. Mind you, there were insurrections from time to time. Hot-headed youths revolting against the army of occupation. But they were quickly subdued by Herod, insuring the gratitude of Rome.

HECKLERS: Boo!

HEROD: *(to Asa, puzzled)* Why do they jeer?

ASA: Perhaps they feel sir, that by catering to such a powerful nation, you were seeking its patronage.

HEROD: Do not their politicians do likewise?

ASA: Point taken. Shall I go on?

HEROD: If you must.

ASA: *(to audience)* Our people drew great solace from the scriptures. And why not? Were we not God's chosen ones, a holy people? And did not God promise that one day our Messiah would come?

PROPHET: For unto us a child is born, unto us a son is given: and the government shall be upon his shoulder: and his name shall be called Wonderful, Counsellor, the Prince of Peace.

HEROD: *(begin to lower status)* "And the government shall be upon His shoulder." Do you not see my dilemma? His shoulder, not mine! Should this prophesy come to pass, I would no longer be king of the Jews....I could not let this happen. No mere babe should topple my throne!

ASA: *(to audience)* I feared for my master's sanity. Day by day he seemed to sink into the abyss of madness.

HEROD: This shall not happen! *(covers face and moans)*

ASA: *(sotto voce to audience, confidentially)* How could he, a Jew, fear the coming of this child of God? This holy babe? Our people had waited so long for the arrival of our holy babe? Our people had waited so long for tha arrival of our Messiah. Our fathers and our fathers' fathers had waited in vain for the coming. Yet, Herod lived each day dreading the glorious event as if it were about to take place momentarily. Strange, unhappy man! *(beat)* Then came an announcement from Rome.

Treatment 1 *(Prophet reads Narrator's part)*
Treatment 2 *(Narrator moves in and replaces Prophet)*

NARRATOR: And it came to pass in those days that there went out a decree from Caesar Augustus, that all the world should be taxed. And all went to be taxed, all to their own cities.

ASA: Caesar was determined to squeeze the last penny from our purses with his hateful tax. However, I must admit that the hordes of travellers to our many cities did generate business.

Treatment 2 *(Joseph and Mary enter through centre aisle during narration.)*

NARRATOR: And Joseph also went up from Galilee, out of the City of Nazareth, into Judaea, into the City of David, which is called Bethlehem (because he was of the house and lineage of David) to be taxed with Mary his espoused wife, being great with child.

ASA: Worship was brisk. The Temple fires burned night and day; the stench of burning fat from the sacrificial lambs hung over Jerusalem. Herod became even more agitated as time went by, the dark and secret devils of his mind giving him no rest. And the crowds still pushed on each family to their own city.

Treatment 2 *(Joseph and Mary move to up stage bench during narration where they form a stage picture with the Babe whom they have picked up, out of sight, on route.)*

NARRATOR: And so it was that, while they were there, the days were accomplished that she should be delivered. And she brought forth her first-born son, and wrapped him in swaddling clothes and laid him in a manger; because there was no room for them in the inn.

Treatment 2 *(Magi enter during Herod's line and stand before Herod, on a lower level, with their backs to audience.)*

HEROD: One day in the midst of this taxation business, three royal visitors from the East requested an audience with me.

ASA: They were distinguished and regal and learned. Herod was flattered that they should seek him out. He was at his most gracious with them. It never hurts to have friends in high places.

HEROD: And then, that which I had come to fear, fell upon me...for they were seeking information. They asked...

Treatment 1   *(Magi lines read by narrator.)*

Treatment 2   *(Magi speak lines that are divided among them.)*

MAGI: Where is He that is born King of the Jews? For we have seen His star in the East, and are come to worship him.

Treatment 2   *(Scribes and Priests enter during Asa line.)*

ASA: Herod summoned the scribes and priests and screamed...

HEROD: *(livid)* Where shall this Christ be born?

ASA: They ran with haste to consult holy scripture and reported their answer thus.

Treatment 1   *(Narrator speaks Scribe's lines.)*

Treatment 2   *(Scribes and Priests speak lines that are divided among them and exit.)*

SCRIBES: In Bethlehem of Judaea. For thus it is written by the prophet: And thou Bethlehem, in the land of Judea, art not the least among the princes of Judea: for out of thee shall come a Governor that shall rule my people Israel.

HEROD: I hid my inner turmoil and returned to my guests and told them what they wanted to know.

ASA: Herod could be charmingly diplomatic when it suited him. Smiling, he sent the wise men on their way to Bethlehem, saying...

HEROD:	*(purrs)* Go and search diligently for the young child; and when ye have found Him, bring me word again, that I may worship Him also.
Treatment 2	*(Magi move to the nativity stage picture, bow, leave gifts, and exit in three different directions)*
ASA:	They never did return. Wise men, indeed. They saw beyond his words and into his heart. Thus they departed, each to his own country by a different route.
HEROD:	*(shouts, livid)* Vipers! Traitors! *(to the audience)* Now, do you understand? I had no choice! Had they returned…but they did not. *(beat)* And so, I commanded that every child under the age of two, dwelling at Bethlehem and the coasts round about, should be put to death. *(defiantly)* And I would do it again if I had to…Asa?
ASA:	Yes, master?
HEROD:	Why is a leader so misunderstood? I did what I thought was best for me and my people, yet I am called cruel and history reports that I died a madman. For the rest of my reign until the day of my death there was no more talk of a holy birth at Bethlehem. So, you see, I was right after all. *(exits)*
ASA:	*(move down into nave or closer to audience and speak to them)* He died raving and riddled with disease. I never did tell him that the Son of God was, indeed, born that blessed night. For I was there, you see, and beheld for myself the Christ Child lying in a manger. I, too, followed the star to Bethlehem and heard that heavenly choir, praising God in the highest.
HEROD:	*(off)* Asa!

ASA: *(calling)* Coming, sir. *(to audience)* Being warned of Herod in a dream, the Baby Jesus was taken to Egypt where he lived until the death of my master. *(The Holy Family exit.)* The Lord God, in His infinite mercy allowed me to stay alive long enough to hear the words of the Man Jesus and follow Him when He started His ministry in Galilee…But, that is another story.

HEROD   *(off)* Asa!

ASA: *(to audience)* Thank you for listening. May the love of the Christ Child dwell in your hearts tonight, tomorrow, and forever. Amen and amen. *(exits)*

                (Immediately following the drama, whether or not this is a communion service, bread and wine could be placed on a table/altar where the Holy Family had been sitting and either partaken at communion or left there for the remainder of the service as a symbol of Christ's presence among us today.)

A Fair Trade

Scott Douglas

Sermon anytime (but February is the traditional Ten Days for Global Justice month) or a discussion starter
Performance time: approximately 10 minutes.

CHARACTERS:

Jesus Morales (*pronounced héy-zoos mo-ráh-lays*)—a Nicaraguan coffee farmer

Mildred—a Canadian woman in her fifties or sixties, a little bit clueless

Walter—a Canadian man in his fifties or sixties, kind of a bumbler

Workers—at least five of them (they can also play the **Co-op Worker**, **Shipper**, **Roaster**, **Retailer**, and **Consumer** or you can increase the cast with different players for these roles)

TREATMENT AND SETTING:

- Props: a bag of coffee, two coffee cups, newspaper, table and two chairs.

- Divide the chancel into two playing areas, one is **Mildred's** kitchen with the table and two chairs. **Jesus Morales** should be seated facing the other playing area which is where **Walter** and the **workers** will perform.

- A fully memorized and staged presentation of this script is, in my opinion, the first choice for this play. However, Jesus has a lot of data to impart so if memorization seems impossible, Jesus and Mildred can do their parts as a staged reading with stools and music stands for scripts (keeping Mildred and Jesus in costume and Jesus' newspaper in the opening scene). For an effective performance, I never recommend hiding scripts. There are follow-up suggestions made by Ten Days for Global Justice (located in Toronto, Ontario) at the end of the play.

- This play could be used as the sermon, as part of the gospel reading, or as a presentation after church. It can easily be adapted to suit a non-church audience.

- One suitable scripture reading is Matthew 20:1–16

— ◆ —

(A man and a woman sit at a typical Canadian breakfast table, drinking coffee. Mildred is wearing a dressing gown and slippers. The man is hidden behind the newspaper he is reading.)

MILDRED: I hope the coffee's not too strong for you this morning, dear. The coffee maker's been acting up again. Of course, some people like strong coffee. Do you remember that restaurant where they sell the ridiculously over-priced coffee? What was the name of that restaurant again? Oh well, I don't suppose it matters....

(Mildred ad libs more morning chit-chat, perhaps including references to members of the congregation. The man behind the newspaper never responds. Finally...)

MILDRED: Walter....Walter! Are you listening to me?

(The man lowers the newspaper to reveal Jesus Morales, a Nicaraguan coffee farmer. He wears work clothes, bare feet, and a cap or straw hat. He smiles.)

JESUS: Buenos dias, señora.

MILDRED: Waah!! You're not Walter. Where's Walter? Where's my husband? Who are you? How did you get here? What are you doing in my kitchen?

JESUS: I have come about your coffee, señora.

MILDRED: My coffee?...Oh, I get it! You're Juan Valdez!

JESUS: No, señora, my name is Jesus Morales...

MILDRED: I've seen all your commercials. Where's your mule?

JESUS: I'm not Juan Valdez! My name is Jesus Morales.

MILDRED: Are you related to Juan?

JESUS: Distant cousin. I am a *cafetelero*, a coffee farmer, from Nicaragua. I have come to you because I've heard that you are a Christian woman, and that you wish to do good in the world.

MILDRED: Well, yes, hubby and I go to church regularly, and try to give to charities and such, but…

JESUS: Then it is very important that you know where your coffee comes from.

MILDRED: I know where my coffee comes from—Safeway, aisle seven. What I want to know is, where has my husband gone?

JESUS: Your husband and I have magically exchanged places. Call it a "fair trade" if you like. I am at your breakfast table, and he is on my coffee farm in Nicaragua.

    (A befuddled Walter, still wearing pajamas, enters a different part of the playing space. He looks around, confused.)

WALTER: Mildred? Mildred, where are you? Have you turned the thermostat up again?

JESUS: Señora, may I tell you a story? It's sort of a parable, like the parable of the workers in the vineyard from the Bible…only completely different. Once upon a time there was a poor *cafetelero* who had a small 3 hectare coffee farm in Nicaragua. (That would be me.)

    (A group of five or six workers, dressed in work clothes, enter and gather around Walter. They welcome him with handshakes, slaps on the back, and calls of "Bienvenidos." As Jesus tells the story, the workers encourage Walter to help them act it out in movement and mime. Play this all for comedy. Poor Walter doesn't know what he's supposed to be doing or why. He can ad lib reactions and commentary

throughout, like "Gosh, this is hard work," or "How long until quitting time?" The workers can have fun getting him to do the work. Walter is always a little behind, trying to catch up.)

JESUS: For three years we've been waiting for the coffee plants to produce fruit. It was hard to survive for those first three years, but finally there are ripe cherries on the branches, and it is time for the harvest. So we climb up the hill to the coffee plants, (which grow only at certain heights), and we pick.

(The workers sling cloth pouches over their shoulders, give one to Walter, and then they climb the hill. Climb, climb, climb. And then they pick "cherries" from the coffee plant at shoulder height or higher. Pick, pick, pick. Jesus waits for them to complete the actions before continuing.)

JESUS: If a rain comes before we have finished picking, the cherries will be washed away, so we must pick quickly. When the pouches are full we take them down the hill where they can be fermented. We then separate the pulp from the bean. The pulp is returned to the soil as compost, while the beans are each washed by hand. It is a very laborious process.

(The workers descend, descend, descend. Dump cherries. Wait. Remove cherries. Grind, grind, grind. Throw compost. Scrub beans. Scrub, scrub, scrub).

JESUS: Now we lay the beans out to dry. If there is a chance of rain, they must all be gathered up and taken inside.

(Spread out beans. One of the workers holds out a hand and checks for rain. She whistles to others, who quickly gather the beans. She whistles again, indicating false alarm, and the beans are spread out again. Walter and the workers are exhausted.)

JESUS:	After two or three days the beans are dry. They can be put in sacks and taken to the co-operative warehouse.

(The workers load a huge sack of beans on Walter's back. They point down the aisle and give him directions.)

WALTER:	What? Where? How far? Fifty kilometers?! On foot?! You've got to be kidding.

(The workers wave goodbye and exit. Walter carries the heavy sack down the aisle to the back of the church.)

JESUS:	You see, although we work very hard, we are very poor. There is no electricity where I live. No telephone, no medical facilities.

MILDRED:	Oh dear, I hope Walter remembered to take his pills. Tell me, Mr. Morales, if coffee doesn't pay very well, why don't you just do something else?

JESUS:	We do grow food for ourselves on the farm, but we also need cash for many of our basic necessities. My country has received loans from richer countries, and in order to pay back our debts we must devote much of our land to cash crops, like coffee, which will be sold to those same rich countries.

(Mildred is about to take a sip of coffee, but stops and pushes the cup away from herself.)

JESUS:	Things used to be worse. There was a time when we could only trade with a few powerful *comerciantes*, intermediaries, who only wanted money for themselves and cared nothing for us. We called them coyotes because they would prey on poor farmers. Now we have a coffee farmer's co-operative and things are a little better. Some day our co-op may have enough money to provide a health clinic or a pharmacy for its members.

(One of the workers enters, wearing a jacket or a different hat to indicate that she is now a Co-op Worker. Walter comes back up the aisle, straining under the sack of beans. The co-op worker smiles and waves as Walter approaches.)

CO-OP WORKER: Good news, friend! Coffee went up three cents on the New York Exchange this morning.

JESUS: From the warehouse, all the sacks of coffee beans are taken by truck to the port.

(Co-op Worker and Walter get in a truck. Walter holds the sack on his lap. Drive, drive, drive, jostle, bump, swerve, screech. Four more workers enter and stand spread out in a line. The one furthest from Walter wears a suit jacket and holds a cup, indicating that he is a Consumer, the next one holds a coffee pot (Retailer), the next one wears a white coat (Roaster). The one closest to Walter wears a captain's cap (Shipper). The Shipper takes the sack and pretends to sort through the beans, throwing out the small ones.)

JESUS: At the port the beans are sifted by size. Only the largest can be exported. We would have more large beans if we used chemicals like other coffee farmers, but the chemicals are unhealthy and harmful to the environment. Once the beans are sifted and put in containers, they are loaded in ships and taken to North America, where they are roasted, ground, packaged, and shipped to the retailers.

(The Shipper carries the sack to the Roaster. The Roaster turns his back, makes hissing and grinding sounds, and then turns back around holding a package of coffee.)

MILDRED: Is roasting a difficult process?

JESUS: You could do it in about twenty minutes in your own oven.

(The Roaster hands the package to the Retailer, who puts it in the pot and turns to the Consumer. He pours into the Consumer's cup.)

RETAILER: Warm up your cup, sir?

CONSUMER: Thank you.

MILDRED: How much is a sack of coffee worth?

JESUS: It depends on the year. Sometimes very little, sometimes very much. Let us say that today a sack might cost $1000. *(The Consumer takes out a wad of bills and hands it to the Retailer. The Retailer takes out a chunk and passes it down the line.)* Each person takes a percentage of the cash.

JESUS: But remember that 25 percent of the money you pay for coffee goes to the retailer. And more than half goes to the big companies that roast and grind and package and market. So by the time the coffee farmer gets paid...

(The stack of money finally gets to Walter, but it is much smaller. He counts the few bills in shock.)

WALTER: Seventy dollars?! For a $1000 sack? After I climbed and picked and de-pulped and washed and dried and carried all those beans?!

(The Shipper, the Roaster, and the Retailer exit. The Co-op Worker gives him a sympathetic look and exits as well. The Consumer puts his arm around Walter's shoulder.)

CONSUMER: Look at it this way, Sancho. If you were making a decent living growing coffee, then everyone would want to do it. And then there'd be a glut on the coffee market and prices would drop to next to nothing. And you wouldn't want that, would you. So cheer up, and remember— your exploitation helps millions of North Americans start the day chipper and alert.

(The Consumer leaves. Walter looks at his little money, depressed.)

JESUS: And then there's the workers to pay.

(The workers joyously return, gather around Walter, take some money, thank Walter, and exit, leaving Walter with only one or two bills. Walter sits, defeated.)

MILDRED: So the roasters and the retailers, who come late in the process and do little work of their own, receive the most reward. That is like the vineyard parable.

JESUS: Except that the vineyard parable is about God's generosity, and this story is about an unjust system that keeps me and my family poor.

MILDRED: *(Takes a sip of coffee.)* Oh dear. This coffee tastes bitter now. Tell me, Mr. Morales, do I have to stop drinking coffee?

JESUS: There is a way that you can have fine quality coffee and I can be fairly paid for my work. It's called the *comercio alternativo*, or Fair Trade. Companies like Bridgehead and Just Us work in co-operation with *cafeteleros* like me, guaranteeing a minimum price that is fair, and helping to improve social conditions in our communities. In return, we take extra care with the beans for the *comercio alternativo*. We send them our finest quality, organically grown beans, because they are in solidarity with us. And it's easy for you, all you have to do is look for a special "Fair Trade Mark" on the package; it tells you that the coffee was grown in co-ops like mine. And anyone can carry this coffee, from community coffee shops here in Canada to large supermarket chains. Many churches invest in Fair Trade because it is a practical way of doing justice in the world; one that allows us to become self-reliant and able to help our own communities. Fair Trade is good for everyone.

MILDRED: Thank you for coming, Mr. Morales. I was a bit disappointed at first, especially when I found out you were neither Juan nor Julio Iglesias, but I've learned a lot from your visit. You certainly have opened my eyes. Thank you.

(Pause. Jesus makes no moves to leave).

MILDRED: Was there something else?

(Jesus points to her cup of coffee)

MILDRED: Oh! Oh. Well, you see, I'd really very much like to buy fairly traded coffee, but, you know how it is, creatures of habit, hubby is attached to the familiar taste of our regular brand.

JESUS: That's fine. I'll just make myself comfortable until you change your mind.

MILDRED: Pardon my asking, but how long were you thinking of staying?

JESUS: Have you heard the expression, "the poor you shall have with you always?"

MILDRED: Always?…Well, I suppose maybe it is time for a change. What did you say the name of that company was? Bridgehead?

JESUS: Señora, you are a good woman, and I have enjoyed our breakfast together, but I must get back to the harvest. Señor? *(Walter looks up.)* Fair trade?

WALTER: Fair trade.

(Jesus and Walter shake hands and switch positions. Jesus exits. Walter kisses Mildred on the cheek, takes a swig of coffee, spits it out, and staggers off, exhausted.)

WALTER: I'm going back to bed.

MILDRED: Well, isn't that typical. Here I am raising my conscious-
                 ness of global economics, and he just wants to sleep in.
                 (Walter and Mildred exit.)

— ◆ —

FOLLOW-UP:

Of course, coffee hour after church would be a great time to hold an in-
formal discussion on people's reactions to the play; given the chance, most
people appreciate an opportunity to ask questions and share their
thoughts. Some enthusiasts suggest holding a coffee taste-test between fair
trade and regular coffee. You could also hold a lunch, a Bible study, or a
viewing of one of the videos suggested in the TEN DAYS resources.

Here are some suggested discussion questions. It's helpful to ask someone to facilitate this discussion, and you might want to have some of the
actors present share their reactions and thoughts:

- What was your reaction to this play? Are there any particular
  feelings or thoughts that come to mind?

- Were there ideas or scenes with which people agreed or disa-
  greed strongly? Ask people if they identified with any of the
  characters or dialogue.

- How does the reality of global trade compare with Jesus'
  words in the Parable of the Workers?

For more information contact

Ten Days for Global Justice
947 Queen Street East, #201
Toronto, ON M4M 1J9

phone: 416-463-5312
fax: 416-463-5569

www.web.net/~tendays
e-mail: tendays@web.net

When I Grow Up

Louise Smith

Meeting discussion starter or portion of sermon
Performance time: 3 minutes

CHARACTERS:
Bobby
Sally
Jimmy
Sam
Mother's off stage voice

TREATMENT:
It is best played by adults or teenagers (playing children) seated on the floor in a semicircle as children would sit. It would be a charming opening to a sermon when the topic was relevant. It would be a great discussion starter for "What is God's job?" or an adult values discussion on the topic "What I might do when I grow up." Have actors wear clothing appropriate for young children.

SETTING:
An elevated central space—no set pieces or props.

— ◆ —

BOBBY:	When I grow up I'm gonna be a police officer.
SALLY:	That's just cause your dad's a police officer.
BOBBY:	Is not.
SALLY:	Is too.
JIMMY:	So. My dad's bigger than your dad. My dad's a fire fighter. An' when I grow up I'm gonna be a fire fighter just like my dad.
BOBBY:	Who says your dad's bigger than my dad?

JIMMY: I says.

SALLY: So. I'm gonna be a nurse. My mom says nurses make the most money.

JIMMY: So. My mom says it's not the money that counts. It's the uniform!

BOBBY: Yeah, it's the uniform. That's why it's best to be a police officer.

SAM: You guys are crazy. Always fightin' over what you're gonna be when you grow up.

JIMMY: So.

BOBBY: Yeah, so.

SALLY: If you're so smart, what're you gonna be?

SAM: Well, I was sittin' in Sunday school the other day an' it really made me think. When I grow up I wanna work for a church.

JIMMY: A church! Why do you want to work for a church?

SAM: Well. I was thinkin'. Every now and then, the women in my church, cook up these great meals. An' I was thinkin', I'd sure get my fair share of yummy suppers if I worked in a church.

BOBBY: No kiddin'?

SAM: No kiddin'. Plus, my teacher told me all about this cool place called heaven. She says it's perfect. I guess you go there when you croak. So, when I'm a goner, I figure I'll get to play as many video games as I want. And no one will tell me to wash my hands before I eat. The way I figure it, workin' in a church would be a sure fire way of gettin' into heaven.

BOBBY: Does any one get to wear a uniform?

SAM: Just the angels, I guess.

BOBBY: Hmm. Ya know, it does sound kinda neat.

SALLY: Can girls be angels? *(Boys all shake their heads no.)*

JIMMY: Know what my dad would say, *(imitating dad's voice)*, "aim for the top Jimmy, aim for the top."

SALLY: What's that supposed to mean?

JIMMY: He'd want me to skip the church thing and go straight for God's job.

   (A voice yells from outside the stage area, calling Sam in for supper.)

SAM: Gotta go guys. See ya tomorrow.

   (The children get up and head out in different directions shouting their goodbyes to each other.)

Spring Again

Spring like a true friend
calls out yes and yes to life
Again and Again

The Quem Quaeritis Trope

Paul Bosch

A 10th century dramatization of the introit for use as an entrance rite
on Easter morning
Performance time: 4 minutes with hymn

CHARACTERS:
Angel
Three Women (the three Marys)
Entire Congregation

TREATMENT AND SETTING:
This is an ancient and formal beginning to an Easter early morning celebration. (See background information on this ancient rite at the bottom of this page.)

   To provide an alternative to the congregation participating in the procession, as described below, the following instructions could be printed in the bulletin, "Our worship this morning begins with a procession with candle, cross, and choir; the congregation is invited to stand in silence, turning to face the processional cross as it enters, and to remain standing for the brief Easter drama. At the end of this six line dialogue, the congregation is invited to join choir and actors in singing, "Jesus Christ Is Risen Today," as the beginning of our worship.

   The congregation gathers in the narthex or hall outside the nave. Inside the nave, all is dark. At the entrance to the nave, in the doorway, stands the paschal candle, lighted now or earlier at the great vigil.

— ◆ —

"Quem quaeritis" is Latin for "Whom do you seek…?" It is the first line of a brief liturgical drama, dating from the nineth century.

   It is called a trope, from the Latin for "turn" (as in "heliotrope": "turning toward the sun"), "turn" is used here in its sense of decoration or embellishment. Liturgical "tropes" were thus decorations or embellishments to liturgical rites, such as matins (morning prayer) or Eucharist. This trope could be thought of as a dramatic elaboration of an Easter introit.

   Tropes were written, in Latin, to be performed by priests or monks, usually "costumed" in vestments, and perhaps sung. Simple stage directions, and perhaps even props such as those suggested above might have elaborated the action.

   In this translation, "Alleluia!" has been substituted for the Latin exclamation in the original.

(A young man—the angel—enters from the dark nave and stands by the paschal candle in the doorway. He is vested and carries a palm branch. As he takes his place, the three Marys come through the congregation to the doorway and stand before the angel. The women are vested in alb and shawl or head scarf. The first two carry a candle holder and candle from the altar. The third carries a thurible or incense pot with incense burning if your congregation is open to this! The Marys speak in unison.)

ADAM: Whom do you seek in the sepulchre, O followers of Christ?

MARYS: Jesus of Nazareth, who was crucified, O Celestial One.

ANGEL: *(Gestures into the darkened nave.)* He is not here. He is risen, as He said.

MARYS: *(Joyously!)* Alleluia! The Lord is risen today! The Strong Lion, Christ the Son of God. Alleluia!

ANGEL: Come and see the place where the Lord was laid. Alleluia! Alleluia!

(The angel turns to a table just inside the doorway, where the white altar cloth lies folded. He picks it up, still folded, and shows it to the Marys. The first Mary gives her candle to the second Mary, and takes the folded cloth from the angel.)

ANGEL: Go quickly, tell the disciples that the Lord is risen indeed. Alleluia! Alleluia!

MARYS: The Lord is risen from the grave, who for us hung on the cross. Alleluia.

(Now the angel carries the paschal candle into the nave, with the Marys, liturgical ministers and congregation following. All sing the processional hymn,

"Jesus Christ Is Risen Today." As the congregation enters with noise-makers and banners, the angel places the paschal candle to the side of the altar or communion table. The Marys dress the altar with the cloth and candles. The congregation moves into the pews and the service continues.)

The Parable of the Talents

Jessica Booker

Scripture and sermon and/or discussion starter
Performance time: 6 to 8 minutes—without discussion

CHARACTERS:
Narrator
Rahab
Haseem
Abdul
1st Voice
2nd Voice
3rd Voice
4th Voice
5th Voice
6th Voice
7th Voice

TREATMENT:
You can reduce 7 voices to 3 voices in rotation for a smaller cast. The **Voices** can enter and exit or be on stage the whole time with backs to the audience until each turns to enter the scene. As an exit they simply turn their backs again. You might have the **Voice's** costume or hat match the costume or hat of the **Servant** to whom they speak to give the appearance of the Voice being the **Servant's** mind. If **Voices** actually enter and exit the space, have them come from different directions to vary the movement.

   The three **Servants** could wear white half masks, (as described in the Workshop section of this book), to show them as elements of universal human character rather than as individuals.

   The Voices could be costumed in loud jackets, sun glasses—whatever suggests smarmy or brash sales people.

   Servant's money and money purse can be mimed or if actual props are used make them theatrically large to be seen from a distance.

SETTING:
One central area where all action can be easily seen.

— ◆ —

NARRATOR: For the realm of heaven is as a person travelling into a far country, who called his own servants and delivered unto them his goods.
And unto one he gave five talents, to another two, and to another one; to every person according to his several ability, and straightway took his journey. (Matt. 25:14–15)

NARRATOR: *(To audience)* We want to present to you our version of the story of the three servants entrusted with their master's money. Their names are not mentioned in the biblical account and so we are taking the liberty of calling them Rahab, Haseem, and Abdul. What thoughts must have raced through their heads as their master left for that far country. Could they live up to his trust in them? Could we? Let us see….

RAHAB: My name is Rahab, chief steward in my master's household. It is my job to see to the smooth running of his estate. Up until now, he has been satisfied.

1ST VOICE: Up until now? What have you done?

RAHAB: He's left me with a problem.

1ST VOICE: Aha! A problem, eh? And just where is your master?

RAHAB: He's gone on a business trip to a far country and will be away a long time.

1ST VOICE: So what's the problem?

RAHAB: See this purse? *(Holds it up.)* It is filled with silver. My master has entrusted it to me…I shall spend it with great care.

1ST VOICE: Friend, this is your lucky day. I just happen to have 10 hectares of prime land near the Dead Sea I can let you have cheap.

RAHAB: Think I was born yesterday? Get away from me. (*1st Voice exits.*)

2ND VOICE: What a rascal that fellow was. Imagine trying to trick a smart chap like you.

RAHAB: Isn't it nice that you're not selling anything.

2ND VOICE: Well, I wouldn't say that…

RAHAB: Oh? Then what do you have in mind?

2ND VOICE: Certainly not arid land, my dear sir.

RAHAB: Well, if my master's money can be well invested, then I'm interested.

2ND VOICE: It may be a little far afield, but you couldn't do better than to purchase a little pyramid I'm selling on the Nile. It's the "in" thing to do, you know. Your master will love it.

RAHAB: Close the door on your way out.

2ND VOICE: You don't know what you're turning down. I just happen to have an end unit left and tomorrow is open house.

RAHAB: Out! Out!

2ND VOICE: I'm going, I'm going…(*Exits*)

3RD VOICE: Psst. Psst. Wanna buy a hot sun dial?

RAHAB: Remove yourself!

3RD VOICE: What a grouch…(*Exits*)

RAHAB: (*To audience*) Someone else's money is a grave responsibility. I shall invest it in a short-term certificate that will yield a safe interest. My master's money will be working for him and I shall have a peaceful mind. (*Exits*)

HASEEM: I am Haseem, second servant in the master's household. I have not been here as long as Rahab—but my master smiles on me with favour…I am a most resourceful fellow.

4TH VOICE: You've got a bit of a swelled head too, haven't you?

HASEEM: If you mean I am vain…say so.

4TH VOICE: You're vain, Haseem.

HASEEM: I have a healthy opinion of myself, friend…and I am ambitious. One day I shall be chief steward when Rahab steps down…

4TH VOICE: Ah, but your master is not here now and we hear that Rahab has been entrusted with a great deal of money.

HASEEM: That is true. But I, too, have some of the master's money….Oh, not as much as was left to Rahab, but a goodly sum, My master will want a reckoning when he returns.

(4th Voice exits.)

5TH VOICE: When he returns…ah, yes. But that won't be for many months. In the meantime, let us eat, drink, and be merry….Let's have a party….You have many friends, Haseem.

HASEEM: It takes much silver to buy food for a party.

5TH VOICE: Which you have, dear boy.

RAHAB: Which I do not have, dear boy. It is not mine to spend.

5TH VOICE: Details…Details…You'll make it up before your master returns.

HASEEM: How do you propose I should do that?

5TH VOICE: Come on…a smart lad like you….You know….You cheat a little here and skimp a little there on paying the tradespeople, and before you know it, you've got it all back….

HASEEM: You seem very experienced at that sort of thing.

5TH VOICE: My boy, I'm an expert….In my last five jobs I've put away a little extra….

HASEEM: In your last five jobs? A fine steward you are. You'll end up being put away yourself, you crook. Now leave—and keep your hands in your pockets.

(*5th Voice exits.*)

ABDUL: Ah, Haseem, there you are. I've been looking for you.

HASEEM: Well you've found me, Abdul. But I cannot stop now. I have just made up my mind about the master's silver. I shall purchase seed and sow the 2 hectares that are not being used by the time the master returns, I should have reaped and sold the crop for him. That should bring a nice return on his money.

ABDUL: Oh, Haseem you are so clever….Why didn't I think of that?

HASEEM: But the master left you only one piece of silver. That plan will not work for you.

ABDUL: (*Dithering*) Then what shall I do?

HASEEM: That is your problem, my friend…I must go. (*Exits*)

ABDUL: Oh, dear…The master is a hard man…. He expects too much of me. This one piece of silver is like a noose around my neck….

6TH VOICE: Abdul—faithful steward—have I got a lottery ticket for you. For only one piece of silver you could become richer than your master.

ABDUL: (*Fascinated*) One piece of silver?

6TH VOICE: Just one little piece of silver and if your ticket is drawn, the riches of a lifetime could be yours.

ABDUL: You make it sound so easy….

6TH VOICE: Easy as falling off a camel.

ABDUL: (*A quivering mass*) Oh dear, I hate making decisions. What shall I do?

6TH VOICE: Make up your mind, pal. I've got other customers waiting.

ABDUL: Here…take the money….no…no…wait. I could lose, too.

6TH VOICE: So what's the worst that could happen if you lost the silver?

ABDUL: The beating of my life….No…no. I can't take a chance like that.

6TH VOICE: Picky….Picky….(*Exits*)

ABDUL: Oh, dear….Oh, dear. What shall I do?

7TH VOICE: I'll be happy to keep that silver coin for you. Hand it over.

ABDUL: (*With terror*) I don't know you….Keep away from me….You want to rob me….

7TH VOICE: The thought had occurred to me….

ABDUL: Help!…Help! (*Runs around madly*)

7TH VOICE: Keep your money....I'm gone....(***Exits***)

ABDUL: (***To audience***) Now I know what I must do.... I'll hide this coin under a bush in the field and when my master comes home, he will see that I have kept it safe for him....That is the best I can come up with....

(***To audience***) What would you do? (***Exits***)

(***Leave a bit of silence to ponder this question.***)

— ◆ —

This play could be followed by discussion, in pairs, in the pews. It could also be used to launch a talent campaign. Possible discussion questions are:

- What is something that I've been told that I do well?
- How could I use this gift more fully?" (Always make it clear that those who do not wish to discuss with a neighbour are free to ponder the questions alone in their own minds.)

Or a fuller discussion could be facilitated during coffee hour following the service.

Launching a talent campaign (submitted by Rev. Robin Wardlaw):

- Invite members of your congregation to raise funds by using their skills and talents.
- Each participant is given 10 or 20 dollars to invest by purchasing supplies for baking, woodworking, babysitting, or some other project.
- On a specified date, everyone brings back the proceeds of their activities to donate to the campaign.

Sun and Moon

Louise Smith

Homily or meeting discussion piece or a dramatic beginning to a seminar on grief
Performance time: 2 minutes

CHARACTERS:
Brother Sun
Sister Moon

TREATMENT AND SETTING:
The two cast members begin at opposite ends of the playing area—emphasizing the distance between the two. With every line the two move closer together, until Brother Sun's final lines, when the two clasp hands with each other.

— • —

BROTHER SUN: You may well say that the sun can't speak. But you also probably thought once that fire wasn't hot or that spinach wasn't good or that your cat wouldn't scratch or that your shoes would stay tied. And maybe you found out differently! Well, on this day, on the day Jesus carried his cross, I spoke. I am Brother Sun.

SISTER MOON: And I am Sister Moon. Whenever my brother sun has cause to speak, I too find myself with voice and words. He speaks of hot, bright, powerful places in our lives.

BROTHER SUN: And she, my sister moon, she speaks of the damp, cool, vulnerable places in our lives. I prefer not to hear her! **(Step away one step.)**

SISTER MOON: But on this day, the day Jesus carried his cross, my brother spoke. And as soon as he spoke, my tongue too was loosed.

205

BROTHER SUN: I said, "Be strong. Bear up under your weight there, do not stumble, do not let them see your tears and your pain."

SISTER MOON: And I said, "Show them your struggle. Let them wipe your face and give you drink, even let them carry your cross for you for a time. Let them hear your cries, otherwise they might think it didn't hurt."

BROTHER SUN: *(Now clasping hands with Sister Moon.)* And my sister taught us all. Only when you admit you have been brought low, is there made room for you to rise.

— ◆ —

Suggested discussion or meditation question:
- When have I felt vulnerable or crucified? Did I grow or did I retreat from that experience?

About the Contributors

Stephen Bemrose-Fetter

Stephen is one of the ministers at Metropolitan United Church in Toronto, Ontario. *Not Just the Pretty Parts* was written to be performed at the Christmas Eve service at Metropolitan in 1996. The drama reflects the kinds of encounters that might occur in that sanctuary during winter afternoons. The play was produced again in 1997 by the John Milton Society's "In Sound" audio tapes for the blind.

Craig S. Boly, S.J.

Craig entered the Society of Jesus in 1962. He obtained a Ph.D. in Theology from the Toronto School of Theology in 1982. He has taught high school English and drama and college theology. *On Death* began as an assignment, a pastoral explanation for the meaning of death, when Craig was studying for the priesthood. A young, chronically ill priest inspired the creation of this drama. Since 1992 he has been pastor of St. Joseph Church, the Jesuit parish in Seattle.

Jessica Booker

Jessica is a widow, grandmother, and professional actor. She is a member of ACTRA, Canadian Actors Equity, and has been a member of St. James Presbyterian Church, in Etobicoke, for forty years. Over the years she has written thirty scripts; two have been published previously. *The Parable of the Talents* was written for a group of youngsters who performed in her drama, *The Bethlehem Story*.

Paul F. Bosch

Born in Buffalo, N.Y., the fifth generation of Lutheran pastors, Paul has spent most of his professional life as a pastor. Paul is devoted to the Gospel and the arts, and sees Christian faith engaging all the arts of worship.

Margaret (Peg) Cox

Margaret grew up in England, but later emigrated to Canada and practised pediatrics for several years. She is retired and lives with her husband in British Columbia. She has four children and four grandchildren. Margaret enjoys writing and since her retirement, she has produced a number of poems, essays, stories, and a play. *First Things First* was a contribution to a July 1995 church service led by the women of the church.

Scott Douglas

Scott is a professional playwright and a staff associate at St. Paul's United Church in Saskatoon. He believes that through drama, congregations are challenged to move, to act, and to be agents of change in the world. *A Fair Trade* was commissioned by Ten Days for Global Justice in 1998. *The Tables Turned and the Stone Gets Rolled Away* was commissioned by the Manitoba and Northwestern Ontario Conference Justice Committee for a Lenten worship resource package on poverty.

Peggy Freeman

Peggy lives in Red Deer, Alberta, and is an active member of St. Luke's Anglican Church. *Jonah* was written for use by the church school while she served as superintendent. The play's large props, such as the six-to-seven-foot long and five-foot high whale, were loved by the children. Peggy won the Stephen Leacock Festival Award in 1993 for her story *Of Bibles, Bluebottles and Broken Hearts*.

Esther E. Harris

Esther is seventy-two years of age, lives in Richmond, B.C., and is a member of St. Alban's Anglican Church. In 1955 Esther and her family emigrated to Canada and from 1961 to 1997 she completed various university degrees and programs. Throughout the years she has had many of her poems and articles published. A women's issues course provided Esther with exciting insights and fresh prespectives on scripture, and, in turn, inspired the creative expression of *At Jacob's Well*.

Jason Heinmiller

Originally from the small town of Fordwich, Ontario, Jason is a member of Fordwich United Church. Jason was 16 years old when the idea for *The Night Lights* popped into his head while cutting grass one day. The play was presented for the first time at his Sunday school's annual Christmas concert that same year. The support received from this play led Jason to write and produce more short plays for community theatre.

barb m. janes

barb has been hooked on theatre since the age of ten, when she was infected by the song, "Another Openin', Another Show" in *Kiss Me, Kate*. Since then, she has acted, written, crewed, produced, directed, and publicized countless shows for churches and community groups. She is beginning a new pastoral relationship with the people of Cloverdale and Selkirk in Manitoba.

Joseph Juknialis

Joseph is a Catholic priest of the Archdicoese of Milwaukee, Wisconsin. He is presently the director of the Preaching Institute at Saint Francis Seminary, director of the college program of Saint Francis Seminary, and associate pastor of SS. Peter and Paul parish. *Bread That Remembers* was written after a Holy Week celebration of the Eucharist at the parish grade school.

David Kai

David is a diaconal minister at Orleans United Church in Orleans, Ontario. *A Holy Week Broadcast* was written for intergenerational worship and is one in a series of dramatic presentations for Palm/Passion Sunday. David grew up as a member of the Centennial-Japanese United Church in Toronto. David and spouse, Marly Bown, live in Orleans with their three children, Tamiko, Michiko, and Mariko.

Gary Paterson

An ordained minister for the past twenty-one years and a father of three daughters, Gary is presently serving at Ryerson United on the west side of Vancouver and is committed to youth and young adult ministry. *The Call of Moses* was created at Soulstice '96, at Naramata, an end of summer event for young adults. Gary and his collaborator, Keri Wehlander, were resource persons for the event; the play was created through the day's theme, "You Can Make a Difference."

Matthew Penny

Matthew is a minister of the United Church in St. Thomas, Ontario. An active writer, Matthew has produced articles and reflections in various publications. As well, he has written services for *The Whole People of God Curriculum* and for many of the churches where he has served. *Bethlehem Cafe* is his latest attempt to put part of the Christian tradition forward for younger generations.

Carolyn Pogue

Carolyn has written articles, poetry, and stories for both children and adults. She feels that drama, painting, sculpture, and music are important for informing the heart and spirit. Recently, Carolyn focused on the women present during the Crucifixion, particularly the mothers. A friend told her about a woman in his congregation whose divorced son kidnapped his own child and fled across the country. When the police closed in, he killed the child and then himself. It was this man's mother who provided the impetus for *Can We Be With Her Too?*

M. Louise Smith

Louise lives in the small Ontario town of Holland Landing with her husband, three children, and two bearded collies. She is an active member of the Holland Landing United Church and at present she directs all drama. Louise has been writing and directing drama for years although she only recently decided to seek publication.

Elizabeth Symon

Originally from England, Elizabeth has been living in Canada for over thirty-five years. She has taught Sunday school in the United Church in the Yukon, the Prairies, Toronto, and British Columbia. Now a grandmother of seven, she lives in Shawnigan Lake on Vancouver Island and attends the local Sylvan United Church. *First Things First* was written three years ago with Peg Cox, her collaborator, on Peg's wisteria-covered verandah.

Betty Radford Turcott

The daughter of a minister, Betty grew up surrounded by the church's work and mission. She is an active member of Faith United, in Courtice, Ontario. Betty believes that the very nature of drama helps worship to come alive. She has been writing and performing dramatic monologues of the women of the Bible for almost twenty years. *Naomi* and *Elizabeth* are just two of the many women of the Bible who come to life as she tells their story in the first person.

Kelly Walker

Kelly lives in Hockley Valley, outside of Toronto. He is a singer, song-writer, recording artist, and the author of two books. *Christmas Proclamation at Midnight* came as a result of a liturgical need to *mark* the sacred night as special in the Anglican parish Christ Church, in Bolton, Ontario. The liturgy is welcomed with a cantor singing this text and announcing the birth of God as human. The litany at the end is followed by the hymn, "O Come All Ye Faithful," as the procession flows into the congregation.

Keri Wehlander

Keri lives in Nanaimo, British Columbia, with her partner, Curtis, and their son, Aidan. Keri co-wrote and performed *The Call of Moses* with Gary Paterson. Keri performed the role of God and Gary performed the role of Moses. With Keri at 5'5" tall and Gary at 6'2", the idea of Moses being taller than God added to the humorous nature of the drama. Presenting this biblical story as a drama was a very effective way of helping people to recognize the "reluctant Moses" within themselves.